SILVER EDIT

Teacher's Edition wi

Interactions 2

READING

Pamela Hartmann

Elaine Kirn

Teacher's Edition by Carol Pineiro

Interactions 2 Reading Teacher's Edition with Tests, Silver Edition

Published by McGraw-Hill ESL/ELT, a business unit of The McGraw-Hill Companies, Inc. 1221 Avenue of the Americas, New York, NY 10020. Copyright © 2007 by The McGraw-Hill Companies, Inc. All rights reserved. No part of this publication may be reproduced or distributed in any form or by any means, or stored in a database or retrieval system, without the prior written consent of The McGraw-Hill Companies, Inc., including, but not limited to, in any network or other electronic storage or transmission, or broadcast for distance learning.

ISBN 13: 978-0-07-328395-1 (Teacher's Edition)
ISBN 10: 0-07-328395-9 (Teacher's Edition)

1 2 3 4 5 6 7 8 9 10 CTF MPM 20 09 08 07

Editorial director: Erik Gundersen
Series editor: Valerie Kelemen
Developmental editor: Karen P. Hazar
Production manager: Juanita Thompson
Production coordinator: Vanessa Nuttry
Cover designer: Robin Locke Monda
Interior designer: Nesbitt Graphics, Inc.

Cover photo: Bob Krist/Corbis

Printed in Singapore

McGraw-Hill

www.esl-elt.mcgraw-hill.com

The *McGraw-Hill* Companies

Table of Contents

Introduction

Student Book Teaching Notes and Answer Keys

Welcome to the Teacher's Edition

The Teacher's Edition of *Interactions/Mosaic* Silver Edition provides support and flexibility to teachers using the *Interactions/Mosaic* Silver Edition 18-book academic skills series. The Teacher's Edition provides step-by-step guidance for implementing each activity in the Student Book. The Teacher's Edition also provides expansion activities with photocopiable masters of select expansion activities, identification of activities that support a Best Practice, valuable notes on content, answer keys, audioscripts, end-of-chapter tests, and placement tests. Each chapter in the Teacher's Edition begins with an overview of the content, vocabulary, and teaching goals in that chapter. Each chapter in the Student Book begins with an engaging photo and related discussion questions that strengthen the educational experience and connect students to the topic.

■ Procedural Notes

The procedural notes are useful for both experienced and new teachers. Experienced teachers can use the bulleted, step-by step procedural notes as a quick guide and refresher before class, while newer or substitute teachers can use the notes as a more extensive guide to assist them in the classroom. The procedural notes guide teachers through each strategy and activity; describe what materials teachers might need for an activity; and help teachers provide context for the activities.

■ Answer Keys

Answer keys are provided for all activities that have definite answers. For items that have multiple correct answers, various possible answers are provided. The answer key follows the procedural note for the relevant activity. Answer keys are also provided for the Chapter Tests and the Placement Tests.

■ Expansion Activities

A number of expansion activities with procedural notes are included in each chapter. These activities offer teachers creative ideas for reinforcing the chapter content while appealing to different learning styles. Activities include games, conversation practice, presentations, and projects. These expansion activities often allow students to practice integrated language skills, not just the skills that the student book focuses on. Some of the expansion activities include photocopiable black line masters included in the back of the book.

■ Content Notes

Where appropriate, content notes are included in the Teacher's Edition. These are notes that might illuminate or enhance a learning point in the activity and might help teachers answer student questions about the content. These notes are provided at the logical point of use, but teachers can decide if and when to use the information in class.

■ Chapter Tests

Each chapter includes a chapter test that was designed to test the vocabulary, reading, writing, grammar, and/or listening strategies taught in the chapter, depending on the language skill strand being used. Teachers can simply copy and distribute the tests, then use the answer keys found in the Teacher's Edition. The purpose of the chapter tests is not only to assess students' understanding of material covered in the chapter but also to give students an idea of how they are doing and what they need to work on. Each chapter test has four parts with items totaling 100 points. Item types include multiple choice, fill-in-the blank, and true/false. Audioscripts are provided when used.

■ Black Line Masters (Photocopiable Masters)

Each chapter includes a number of expansion activities with black line masters, or master worksheets, that teachers can copy and distribute. These activities and black line masters are optional. They can help reinforce and expand on chapter material in an engaging way. Activities include games;

conversation practice; working with manipulatives such as sentence strips; projects; and presentations. Procedural notes and answer keys (when applicable) are provided in the Teacher's Edition.

- **Placement Tests**

  Each of the four language skill strands has a placement test designed to help assess in which level the student belongs. Each test has been constructed to be given in under an hour. Be sure to go over the directions and answer any questions before the test begins. Students are instructed not to ask questions once the test begins. Following each placement test, you'll find a scoring placement key that suggests the appropriate book to be used based on the number of items answered correctly. Teachers should use judgment in placing students and selecting texts.

The Interactions/Mosaic Silver Edition Program

Interactions/Mosaic Silver Edition is a fully-integrated, 18-book academic skills series. Language proficiencies are articulated from the beginning through advanced levels <u>within</u> each of the four language skill strands. Chapter themes articulate <u>across</u> the four skill strands to systematically recycle content, vocabulary, and grammar.

- **Reading Strand**

  Reading skills and strategies are strategically presented and practiced through a variety of themes and reading genres in the five Reading books. Pre-reading, reading, and post-reading activities include strategies and activities that aid comprehension, build vocabulary, and prepare students for academic success. Each chapter includes at least two readings that center around the same theme, allowing students to deepen their understanding of a topic and command of vocabulary related to that topic. Readings include magazine articles, textbook passages, essays, letters, and website articles. They explore, and guide the student to explore, stimulating topics. Vocabulary is presented before each reading and is built on throughout the chapter. High-frequency words and words from the Academic Word List are focused on and pointed out with asterisks (*) in each chapter's Self-Assessment Log.

- **Listening/Speaking Strand**

  A variety of listening input, including lectures, academic discussions, and conversations help students explore stimulating topics in the five Listening/Speaking books. Activities associated with the listening input, such as pre-listening tasks, systematically guide students through strategies and critical thinking skills that help prepare them for academic achievement. In the Interactions books, the activities are coupled with instructional photos featuring a cast of engaging, multi-ethnic students participating in North American college life. Across the strand, lectures and dialogues are broken down into manageable parts giving students an opportunity to predict, identify main ideas, and effectively manage lengthy input. Questions, guided discussion activities, and structured pair and group work stimulate interest and interaction among students, often culminating in organizing their information and ideas in a graphic organizer, writing, and/or making a presentation to the class. Pronunciation is highlighted in every chapter, an aid to improving both listening comprehension and speaking fluency. Enhanced focus on vocabulary building is developed throughout and a list of target words for each chapter is provided so students can interact meaningfully with the material. Finally, Online Learning Center features MP3 files from the Student Book audio program for students to download onto portable digital audio players.

- **Writing Strand**

  Activities in each of the four Writing books are systematically structured to culminate in a *Writing Product* task. Activities build on key elements of writing from sentence development to writing single paragraphs, articles, narratives, and essays of multiple lengths and genres. Connections between writing and grammar tie the writing skill in focus with the grammar structures needed to develop each writing skill. Academic themes, activities, writing topics, vocabulary development, and critical thinking strategies prepare students for university life. Instructional photos are used to strengthen engagement and the educational experience. Explicit pre-writing questions and discussions activate prior knowledge, help organize ideas and information, and create a foundation for the writing product. Each chapter includes a self-evaluation rubric which supports the learner as he or she builds confidence and autonomy in academic writing. Finally, the Writing Articulation Chart helps teachers see the progression of writing strategies both in terms of mechanics and writing genres.

■ Grammar Strand

Questions and topical quotes in the four Grammar books, coupled with instructional photos stimulate interest, activate prior knowledge, and launch the topic of each chapter. Engaging academic topics provide context for the grammar and stimulate interest in content as well as grammar. A variety of activity types, including individual, pair, and group work, allow students to build grammar skills and use the grammar they are learning in activities that cultivate critical thinking skills. Students can refer to grammar charts to review or learn the form and function of each grammar point. These charts are numbered sequentially, formatted consistently, and indexed systematically, providing lifelong reference value for students.

■ Focus on Testing for the TOEFL® iBT

The all-new TOEFL® iBT *Focus on Testing* sections prepare students for success on the TOEFL® iBT by presenting and practicing specific strategies for each language skill area. The Focus on Testing sections are introduced in Interactions 1 and are included in all subsequent levels of the Reading, Listening/Speaking, and Writing strands. These strategies focus on what The Educational Testing Service (ETS) has identified as the target skills in each language skill area. For example, "reading for basic comprehension" (identifying the main idea, understanding pronoun reference) is a target reading skill and is presented and practiced in one or more *Focus on Testing* sections. In addition, this and other target skills are presented and practiced in chapter components outside the *Focus on Testing* sections and have special relevance to the TOEFL® iBT. For example, note-taking is an important test-taking strategy, particularly in the listening section of the TOEFL® iBT, and is included in activities within each of the Listening/Speaking books. All but two of the *Interactions/Mosaic* titles have a *Focus on Testing* section. Although *Interactions Access Reading* and *Interaction Access Listening/Speaking* don't include these sections because of their level, they do present and develop skills that will prepare students for the TOEFL® iBT.

■ Best Practices

In each chapter of this Teacher's Edition, you'll find Best Practices boxes that highlight a particular activity and show how this activity is tied to a particular Best Practice. The Interactions/Mosaic Silver Edition team of writers, editors, and teacher consultants has identified the following six interconnected Best Practices.

---

* TOEFL is a registered trademark of Educational Testing Services (ETS). This publication is not endorsed or approved by ETS.

Best Practices

Each chapter identifies at least six different activities that support six Best Practices, principles that contribute to excellent language teaching and learning. Identifying Best Practices helps teachers to see, and make explicit for students, how a particular activity will aid the learning process.

Making Use of Academic Content

Materials and tasks based on academic content and experiences give learning real purpose. Students explore real world issues, discuss academic topics, and study content-based and thematic materials.

Organizing Information

Students learn to organize thoughts and notes through a variety of graphic organizers that accommodate diverse learning and thinking styles.

Scaffolding Instruction

A scaffold is a physical structure that facilitates construction of a building. Similarly, scaffolding instruction is a tool used to facilitate language learning in the form of predictable and flexible tasks. Some examples include oral or written modeling by the teacher or students, placing information in a larger framework, and reinterpretation.

Activating Prior Knowledge

Students can better understand new spoken or written material when they connect to the content. Activating prior knowledge allows students to tap into what they already know, building on this knowledge, and stirring a curiosity for more knowledge.

Interacting with Others

Activities that promote human interaction in pair work, small group work, and whole class activities present opportunities for real world contact and real world use of language.

Cultivating Critical Thinking

Strategies for critical thinking are taught explicitly. Students learn tools that promote critical thinking skills crucial to success in the academic world.

1

Education and Student Life

In this chapter, students will read about education and how different values of a society are reflected in different educational practices. They will learn about contrasts in schooling in Mexico, Japan, the U.K., and the United States, and how these differences prepare students to continue certain aspects of culture and tradition. A related reading is on the number of foreign students in the United States compared to the number of American students abroad and what their majors are. Another passage is about characteristics of the current generation of students in the United States and the previous generations of the 1960s, 1970s, and 1980s. Finally, a recent topic in academic circles is the use of "politically correct" terminology, which is contrasted to that used a few decades ago. These readings allow students to think about how educational systems both reflect and preserve cultures, providing a powerful tool that guarantees the transmission of values and traditions to future generations.

Chapter Opener

❑ Direct students' attention to the photo on page 3 of the Student Book and ask questions: *Whom do you see? Where are they? What are they doing?*

❑ Read the Chinese proverb and ask students what they think it means.

❑ Put this sentence on the board: *Education in my country is the same as/ different from education in the United States because* _____.

❑ Put students in pairs to discuss the sentence and find several words or phrases to put in the blanks.

❑ Call on students to share their ideas with the class.

❝ If you are planning for a year, sow rice; if you are planning for a decade, plant trees; if you are planning for a lifetime, educate people. ❞

—Chinese proverb

Chapter Overview

Reading Selections

Education: A Reflection on Society

Campus Life is Changing

Reading Skills and Strategies

Previewing the topic and vocabulary

Identifying the topic and main idea

Skimming for the topic and main idea

Predicting content of a reading

Critical Thinking Skills

Interpreting a photograph

Relating a reading passage to a broader world view

Summarizing a paragraph

Organizing information using a T-Chart

Vocabulary Building

Getting meaning from context: punctuation, other sentences, logic

Practicing new vocabulary

Identifying words and phrases that work together

Using prepositions

Focusing on the Academic Word List

Language Skills

Understanding pronoun reference

Discussing student life in different countries

Writing a paragraph

Focus on Testing TOEFL® IBT

Focusing on question types

Vocabulary

Nouns		Verbs	Adjectives	Idioms
aspects*	methods*	afford	compulsory	on the one hand
assignments*	native people	determines	creative*	on the other hand
constitution*	primary* school	involves*	cultural*	
contrasts*	secondary school	lectures*	egalitarian	
culture*	statistic	reflects	entire	
discipline	status*		rural	
goals*	traditions*		universal	
indigenous people	tuition		vocational	
individualism*	values			

*These words are from the Academic Word List. For more information on this list, see www.vuw.ac.nz/lals/research/awl.

Education: A Reflection of Society

Before You Read

1 Previewing the Topic

- ❏ Put students in small groups and have them look at the photos. Tell them to practice asking and answering the questions.

- ❏ Call on students to share their answers with the class. Their answers may vary.

- ❏ Write a few comments they may have about the photos on the board. If there are students from those countries in class, ask them to add their comments.

REPRODUCIBLE — EXPANSION ACTIVITY

- ■ Photocopy and distribute **Black Line Master 1** "Can You Tell Me About Your Schooling?" on page BLM1 of this Teacher's Edition.

- ■ Model the activity. Call on a student and ask *"Did you go to elementary school in a city, town or country?" "Was it public or private?"* Point out that they should write their partner's answers on the paper.

- ■ Divide the students into pairs of students from different countries or regions, if possible.

- ■ Write the beginning and ending time on the board. Students should be able to complete this activity in 10–15 minutes.

- ■ Walk around the room and help students with the questions, if necessary.

- ■ At the end of the time limit, ask the pairs of students to introduce each other to the class.

2 Previewing Vocabulary

- ❏ Read the directions to the students.

- ❏ Have them put a check (✓) next to the words they know.

- ❏ Tell them **not** to use a dictionary during this part of the lesson.

- ❏ Play the audio.

Strategy

Getting Meaning from Context

- ■ On the board, put the phrase *Clues to Meaning*. Under it, write the following punctuation marks (words and symbols) and expressions:

  parentheses ( ) dash — comma ,

  - ■ Another sentence before or after the word or phrase may help.

  - ■ Logic may also help you guess.

- ■ Tell students to look for these punctuation marks and clues when they see words or phrases they don't understand. These clues to meaning will help them understand new words and phrases. Read the examples and explain further if necessary.

3 Getting Meaning from Context

- ❏ Tell students to do the activity.

- ❏ If students finish quickly, have them compare their answers with a partner.

ANSWER KEY

1. on the one hand = *one point of view*
   on the other hand = *another point of view*

2. compulsory = *required*
   universal = *available to everyone*
   primary school = *elementary school*

3. rural = *country*

4. egalitarian = *equal*

5. discipline = *self-control*

6. entire = *whole*
   status = *social position*

7. determines = *decides*

Read

4 Reading an Article

- ❏ Write *"What can we learn about a culture from its educational system?"* on the board and ask students to think about this question as they are reading.

- ❏ Have students read the passage silently within a time limit (10–15 minutes) or have students follow along silently as you play the audio.

- ❏ Tell them to underline any words or phrases that are new or that they don't understand. Remind them **not** to use a dictionary during this part of the lesson.

- ❏ Tell students to read the Strategy Box: **Identifying the Main Idea**, page 9 if they finish before the other students.

Strategy

Identifying the Main Idea

- ■ Call on a student to read out the information in the Strategy Box.

5 Identifying the Main Idea

- ❏ Read the directions and have the students look at Paragraphs A & F and write down the main idea.

- ❏ Give students a time limit of 10–15 minutes.

- ❏ If students finish quickly, have them compare their answers with a partner.

ANSWER KEY

From Paragraph A: The educational system is a mirror that reflects the culture.

From Paragraph F: It is clear that each educational system is a reflection of the larger culture—both positive and negative aspects of its economy, values, and social structure.

6 Understanding Reading Structure

- ❏ Read the directions. Tell students to look back at the reading on pages 7–8 and match the paragraphs with their topics.

- ❏ Check the answers when students finish.

ANSWER KEY

1. F 2. C 3. E 4. B 5. D 6. A

7 Checking Your Vocabulary

- ❏ Read the directions. Remind students **not** to use a dictionary during this part of the lesson.

- ❏ Check the answers when students finish.

ANSWER KEY

1. constitution 2. native/indigenous people
3. isolated 4. vocational 5. afford 6. tuition
7. aspects

Strategy

Organizing Information: Using a *T-Chart*

- ■ Point out the words and expressions that are highlighted in the Strategy Box that show contrasting viewpoints.

- ■ Ask the students to repeat them after you.

Britain	Education is free; egalitarian first 9 years; universities are free; graduates of good universities get best jobs	Students are divided into 3 different groups at age 11 after exam; only 1% of lower class go to university; half of Oxford/ Cambridge students are from upper class
United States	Primary and secondary education is free; 80% finish high school; students decide on college or vocational classes; 60% attend college; adults also attend college	Schools not equal; problems in high schools; schools in poor areas get less money, don't have good teachers or equipment

8   Organizing Information: Using a T-Chart

Best Practice

Organizing Information

Activities such as this will teach students to organize information from a reading passage using a graphic organizer called a T-chart. Using the chart allows students to better assimilate and recall information at a later date, making it a valuable study tool. In this case, students identify positive and negative aspects of the educational systems of the four countries mentioned in the reading.

❑   Read the directions. Divide the students into groups of four and have each student in the group choose a different country. Tell them to fill in the T-chart.

❑   Give students a time limit (10–15 minutes), and check the answers with the whole class when everyone has finished.

ANSWER KEY

Answers may vary.

	Positive Aspects	**Negative Aspects**
Mexico	Education is free, compulsory, universal; supports national unity; leads to improvement of people	Difficult to provide in rural areas; not enough schools or teachers; some Indian groups do not send children to school
Japan	Education is free and egalitarian; 88% finish high school; children with high test scores bring high status to family	Students need discipline; must give up hobbies, sports, social life to study for exams

9 Discussing the Reading

Best Practice

Activating Prior Knowledge

Activities such as this will connect new concepts to students' prior knowledge. By making connections between the text, "Education: A Reflection of Society," and their own experiences, students will be better able to understand the reading and reflect on their own schooling in light of it. By working in a small group, students will help each other make those connections and learn from the group. Finally, by presenting their conclusions to the class, they will share their knowledge and culture with others.

❏ Divide the students into small groups from the same country or region, if possible.

❏ Have the students read the questions on page 11 and write brief answers.

❏ When they finish, ask them to go to the board and make an outline of their school system, or put the outline on a chart.

❏ Have students give a short presentation to the class. Those in the audience can ask questions at the end. Hang the charts around the classroom when students are finished.

Campus Life is Changing

Before You Read

Strategy

Skimming for the Topic and Main Idea

- Explain the difference between the topic and main idea of a paragraph with the information from the Strategy Box.

- Read the example passage in the Strategy Box aloud to the students or call on different students to read a few sentences.

- Ask the students to tell you the topic and the main idea.

Example

Topic: The U.S. college population

Main idea: There are fewer foreign students in the United States these days, but more U.S. students abroad.

Read

1 Skimming for the Topic and the Main Idea

- Tell students to read the paragraphs quickly and write the topic and main idea of each paragraph.

- Remind them **not** to use a dictionary.

- Play the audio.

- Have students check their answers with a partner if they finish quickly.

ANSWER KEY

Answers may vary.

[A] Topic: Changes in U.S. college population

Main Idea: Traditional college students are being replaced by nontraditional students who have different needs and expectations of colleges.

[B] Topic: Learning styles of nontraditional students

Main Idea: Nontraditional students prefer the *sensing* style of learning, or getting experience first and ideas later.

[C] Topic: Learning styles of traditional students

Main Idea: Traditional students prefer the *intuitive* style of learning, or getting theory before practice.

[D] Topic: Preference of college professors

Main Idea: Most college professors prefer the *intuitive* style, so nontraditional, or *sensing*, students are at a disadvantage.

[E] Topic: Changes in interests of students

Main Idea: Students went from being politically active to being interested in making money, but now they are a combination of the two.

[F] Topic: Changes in technology on campus

Main Idea: Advances in technology allow students to perform many tasks online, for example, send applications, register, take classes, do research, take exams, and contact professors.

After You Read

UNDERSTANDING PRONOUN REFERENCE

- Explain the difference between nouns (the name of a person, place or thing) and pronouns (word that takes the place of a person, place or thing). For example,

  boy = he   girl = she
  chair = it   cars = they
  we/you

- Write this list on the board or read it aloud and ask students to tell you if the words are nouns or pronouns.

all *	others *
campus	philosophy
classes	professor
each *	religion
entertainment	science
graduation	she *
he *	someone
his *	style
Internet	technology
it *	them *
jobs	these *
museums	they *
none *	training
ones *	whose *
* = pronouns	

- Explain that in sentences and paragraphs, pronouns *refer to* nouns that come before them. These nouns are called *referents*, and it's important to locate them in a previous sentence or paragraph to understand what the reading is about.

- Look at the information in the box on page 15 and read the example.

2   Understanding Pronoun Reference

- ❏ Have students work individually to complete the activity.

ANSWER KEY

1. they = undergraduate students
2. they = nontraditional students
3. them = nontraditional students
4. their = students in the *sensing* group
5. their = students in the 1980s
6. them = professors

3 Discussing the Reading

> **Best Practice**
>
> **Scaffolding Instruction**
>
> This activity uses the students' prior knowledge as a scaffold. It will help them place what they already know about their own educational system or campus life into the larger framework introduced in the reading on "Campus Life is Changing" on pages 13–15. They will engage in "reinterpretation" or critical thinking about this topic as they formulate ideas with their classmates and give a presentation to the class.

❏ This activity can be conducted like **9 Discussing the Reading** on page 11, forming another part of the project on educational systems in different countries.

❏ Divide the students into small groups from the same country or region, if possible.

❏ Have the students read the questions on page 16 and write brief answers.

❏ When they finish, ask them to go to the board and make an outline of campus life and students in their country, or put the outline on a chart.

❏ Have students give a short presentation to the class. Those in the audience can ask questions at the end. Hang the charts around the classroom when students are finished.

Responding in Writing

Strategy

Summarizing

- Ask a student to read the explanation in the Strategy Box.

4 Summarizing

- ❑ Have the students turn to the reading on pages 6–8 in Part 1.

- ❑ Ask them to skim the paragraph on Mexico again.

- ❑ Then have them look at the T-chart on page 11 listing the positive and negative aspects of Mexico's educational system. These aspects are repeated below.

POSITIVE AND NEGATIVE ASPECTS

Education is free, compulsory, universal; supports national unity; leads to improvement of people

Difficult to provide in rural areas; not enough schools or teachers; some Indian groups do not send children to school

- Elicit a <u>main idea</u> from students and write it on the board.

- Elicit the positive and negative aspects from the students and write them in coherent sentences on the board. Your summary may look like this:

  > <u>In Mexico, education has both positive and negative aspects</u>. On the one hand, it is free, compulsory, and universal, principles that support national unity and lead to the improvement of society. On the other hand, providing good education in rural areas is difficult because there are not enough schools or teachers. In addition, some Indian groups do not send their children to school, which works against national unity and the improvement of some social classes.

- Now have students choose a different country from the reading in Part 1, pages 6–8

- Remind the students to look at the guidelines on page 16 and not to look at the original paragraph as they write.

- When students finish, have them compare their summary with those of other students who summarized the same country.

5 Writing Your Own Ideas

Best Practice

Making Use of Academic Content

Activities such as developing a model for students enable them to be more successful when they work independently. With the teacher's guidance, the students are able to contribute to the summary on the board. Then they are better equipped to write a summary by themselves.

- ❑ Read the topics aloud and ask who is going to write about each topic.

- ❑ Have students write the <u>main idea</u> and underline it. Go around the classroom and check the sentences. Then have them write the rest of the paragraph.

- ❑ Give students 10–15 minutes for this activity. Collect their summaries when they have finished.

Talk It Over

Best Practice

Cultivating Critical Thinking

Activities such as this prepare the students for discussing real-world issues. By including topics like politically correct terminology in the classroom, students become more familiar with North American culture and more prepared to deal with it.

UNDERSTANDING "POLITICALLY CORRECT" LANGUAGE

- Have students look at the passage on page 11 on "Education in North America and Asia."

- Elicit characteristics of students educated in North America. Your students might give answers like *individualism, independent thinking, finding answers by themselves,* or *expressing ideas in a discussion.*

- Tell students that this respect for individualism and differences is part of the reason for using politically correct (PC) terms today.

- Have students repeat both lists of terms after you.

- Use the questions in the directions to begin a class discussion. Ask students if there are similar PC terms in their language.

- If there is time, have pairs of students go to the board and write sentences. One will use the less PC terms, and the other will use PC terms. For example,

  The blind student couldn't cross the street.

  The visually challenged student couldn't cross the street.

- Have them read the sentences when they finish. Ask them how they feel about using the different terms.

6 Beyond the Text: Interviewing

 REPRODUCIBLE **EXPANSION ACTIVITY**

- Photocopy and distribute **Black Line Master 2** "Can You Tell Me Your Opinion?" on page BLM2 of this Teacher's Edition.

- Model the activity. Call on a student and say *"Hello. My name is . . . , and I'm interviewing people for a class assignment. Can you tell me your opinion about the positive aspects of the educational system in your country? How about the negative aspects?"*

- Tell students they should write the person's answers on the paper.

- Give students a few days to complete this assignment.

- When it is finished, elicit answers from students in a large group format. Write the countries not discussed in the chapter readings on the board with positive and negative aspects of each.

1 Focusing on Words from the Academic Word List

❑ Read the directions to students.

❑ Say the words in the list and ask students to repeat them and tell you what form the word is in (noun, verb, adjective, or adverb).

assignments n.	culture n.	lectures v.
contrast n.	goals n.	methods n.
cultural adj.	individualism n.	traditions n.

❑ Tell them to begin the activity and check answers when they have finished.

ANSWER KEY

1. cultural 2. individualism 3. contrast 4. culture
5. goals 6. traditions 7. assignments 8. methods
9. lectures

2 Recognizing Word Meanings

❑ Read the directions.

❑ Remind the students **not** to use a dictionary during this activity.

❑ Check the answers when students have finished.

ANSWER KEY

1. h 2. i 3. j 4. a 5. b 6. e 7. f 8. c 9. l 10. k
11. g 12. d

3 Words in Phrases

❑ Read the directions.

❑ Tell students that they should keep a vocabulary notebook of new words with a special section for words in phrases. They should review this vocabulary every week.

ANSWER KEY

1. in/on 2. attend 3. to 4. at 5. in 6. of 7. to
8. take

4 Searching the Internet

EXPANSION ACTIVITY

■ Photocopy and distribute **Black Line Master 3** "Find A College Or University That…" on page BLM3 of this Teacher's Edition.

■ Take the students to the computer lab or give them instructions for going by themselves.

■ Point out that they should work on this assignment in pairs and then share the information with another pair of students.

■ Tell them to write down the name of the college or university, its location, and its web address (URL) so that other students can find it. For example, *Boston University, Boston, MA/USA www.bu.edu*.

READING QUESTION TYPES

- Read the information in **Reading Question Types**, and call on different students to read the three types of questions.

- Put the following three examples of iBT question types on the board.

---

1   **Practice**

- ❏   Point out the examples of each type in the **Practice** and tell students to turn to pages 6–8 and find the answers.

ANSWER KEY

1. a   2. c   3. d

Self-Assessment Log

- ❏   Explain to students that thinking about their learning can help them decide what to focus on in their lessons and homework and help them chart their progress.

- ❏   The Self-Assessment Log at the end of each chapter helps students track their own strengths and weaknesses and also encourages them to take ownership of their own learning.

- ❏   Read the directions aloud and have students check vocabulary they learned in the chapter and are prepared to use.

- ❏   Have the students check the strategies practiced in the chapter (or the degree to which they learned them). They have actually used all these strategies in Chapter 1.

- ❏   Put students in small groups. Ask students to find the information or an activity related to each strategy in the chapter.

- ❏   Tell students to find definitions in the chapter for any words they did not check.

- ❏   If possible, meet privately with each student on a regular basis and review his or her assessment log. This provides an opportunity for the student to ask key questions and for you to see where additional help may be needed and to offer one-on-one encouragement.

Best Practice

Interacting with Others

Activities such as this will energize the students and add excitement to the class. Since most interaction in this chapter has been dialogic or collaborative, they will enjoy a change of pace with some competitive interaction.

 EXPANSION ACTIVITY

- Tell the students to study the vocabulary for a few minutes in pairs, asking each other to spell the words aloud. Tell them they'll have a test in a few minutes.

- Instruct the students to close their books. Divide them into two teams, balanced for differences like level of English, first language, culture, and gender.

- Have them go to the board, if possible, one by one. Depending on how many students there are in the class, dictate 1–2 words/phrases to each student.

- At the end of the dictation, check the board. Ask students from the other team if the words are spelled correctly. Give them a point for each correct word.

- Tally the score at the end. The team with the highest score wins.

- If it's not possible for the students to go to the board, tell them to write the answers on a sheet of paper.

- Collect the tests and grade them. The team with the highest average score wins.

2

City Life

In this chapter, students will read about different aspects of city life, some positive and some negative. In the first reading, they will learn about an architect who became mayor of Curitiba, a small city in Brazil. Although Brazil is a country of medium development, that is, between a developing and developed country, its cities still have many problems. Students will discover how the new mayor turned Curitiba into a model city that other leaders around the world have tried to emulate. In the second reading, students will learn about a phenomenon called "sick building syndrome" that often occurs in cities. Indoor air pollution causes the people inside buildings to become ill. Students will learn about solutions to this problem, which include removing pollutants and bringing in plants that can extract dangerous chemicals from the air. These topics will encourage students to think about how life in the city can be improved so that people are able to live in increasing comfort and safety.

Chapter Opener

❑ Direct students' attention to the photo on page 23 of the Student Book and ask questions: *What do you see? Where do you think this is? What are the people doing? What kind of life do you think they live? How does city life compare with country life?*

❑ Read the quotation by Jacobsen and ask students what it means.

❑ Put this sentence on the board: *Life in the city is more/less _____ than life in the country.*

❑ Put students in pairs to find several words or phrases to put in the blanks.

❑ Call on students to share their words with the class.

❝ When you look at a city, it's like reading the hopes, aspirations, and pride of everyone who built it. ❞

—Hugh Newell Jacobsen
U.S. Architect (1929–)

Chapter Overview

Reading Selections

A City That's Doing Something Right

Sick–Building Syndrome

Reading Skills and Strategies

Previewing the topic and vocabulary

Identifying the main idea

Identifying supporting details

Predicting content of a reading

Skimming for the topic and the main ideas

Scanning

Critical Thinking Skills

Organizing details using a graphic organizer

Making inferences

Summarizing a paragraph

Understanding contrast

Vocabulary Building

Getting meaning from context: examples, opposite, & *in other words*

Understanding the meaning of italics in readings

Focusing on the Academic Word List

Understanding and looking up parts of speech in a dictionary

Language Skills

Understanding pronoun reference

Interviewing students about city life

Discussing some problems and solutions in big cities

Writing a paragraph

Focus on Testing

Getting meaning from context

Vocabulary

Nouns		Verbs	Adjectives	Adverb	Preposition
access*	pollution	commute	affluent	efficiently	under*
agricultural operation	priorities	crowd	creative*		
crops	produce	cultivate	global*		
developing countries	recycling plant	established*			
environment*	residents*	focus*			
gridlock	transportation*	predict*			
income*	trash	solve			
mass transit	urban dwellers	worsening			
method*					

*These words are from the Academic Word List. For more information on this list, see www.vuw.ac.nz/lals/research/awl.

A City That's Doing Something Right

Before You Read

1   Previewing the Topic

❑ Put students in pairs and have them look at the photos.

❑ Have students read the questions on page 24 and discuss the answers with their partner. Tell them to write adjectives to describe the photos.

❑ Call on students to share their answers with the class.

❑ Write some of the adjectives on the board and discuss their meaning.

2   Thinking Ahead

❑ Read the directions to the students.

❑ Give them a time limit for the activity (10–15 minutes).

❑ When they finish, have them sit down and ask them to share their answers with the class.

❑ Write the names of their cities on the board.

❑ Write down a few of the worst problems and best features.

❑ Point out that their lists are probably similar because many cities have similar problems and attractions.

3   Previewing Vocabulary

❑ Read the directions to the students.

❑ Have them put a check (✓) next to the words they know.

❑ Remind them **not** to use a dictionary during this part of the lesson.

❑ Tell them to put the stress on words of more than one syllable as they listen to the audio program.

❑ Write these words on the board as examples: *grid'lock, predict', ac'tually*

❑ Play the audio.

❑ Have the students write the words with the stress marked on the board.

ANSWER KEY

Nouns	Verbs
agricul'tural operation	commute'
crops	crowd
deve'loping countries	cul'tivate
dif'ficulties (dif'ficulty)	predict'
grid'lock	solve
mass tran'sit	wor'sening
pedes'trian zone	
pollu'tion	**Adjectives**
prio'rities	af'fluent
pro'duce	crea'tive
recyc'ling plant	
trash	**Adverb**
ur'ban dwellers	effic'iently

PRONUNCIATION NOTE

■ Students may be able to repeat words correctly after the audio, but in order for them to remember the pronunciation, tell them to mark the stress as they listen. Later when they practice on their own, they will be able to pronounce the words correctly.

Strategy

Getting Meaning from Context

■ On the board, put the phrase *Clues to Meaning*. Under it, write the following words:

1. *for example,*
   for instance   > introduce examples
   such as
   among them

2. opposite meaning of a new word

3. *that is*   > introduce a definition
   in other words   or explanation

- ■ Call on different students to read each clue and example in the box.

- ■ Tell students to look for these new clues to meaning when they see words or phrases they don't understand. These clues to meaning will help them understand new words and phrases.

4 Getting Meaning from Context

- ❑ Read the directions and the first example.
- ❑ Have students complete the activity individually.

ANSWER KEY

1. predict = say in advance that something will happen
   developing countries = India and Nigeria
2. gridlock = traffic that doesn't move
   commute = go from home to work and back
3. affluent = rich
4. priorities = list of what was most important
5. trash = garbage
6. produce = fruits and vegetables (oranges or potatoes)
7. recycling plant = factory or place where glass bottles, plastic, and cans are made into new products
8. mass-transit = a system of transportation for many people
9. agricultural operation = farm
   crops = plants that produce food (grain, fruit, vegetables)
10. cultivate = grow
11. urban dwellers = city people

Read

5 Reading an Article

- ❑ Write *"What is the city Curitiba, Brazil, doing right?"* on the board and ask students to think about this question as they are reading.

- ❑ Have the students read the passage silently within a time limit (10–15 minutes), or have them follow along as you play the audio.

- ❑ Tell them to underline any words or phrases that are new or that they don't understand. Remind them **not** to use a dictionary during this part of the lesson.

- ❑ Tell students to look at activity **6 Recognizing the Main Idea** if they finish the reading.

- ❑ Start the audio.

After You Read

IDENTIFYING THE MAIN IDEA

- ■ Call on a student to read the information in the box to remind them about the main idea.

6 Identifying the Main Idea

- ❑ Read the directions and give the students a few minutes to find the main idea in Paragraphs B and G.

- ❑ Tell students who have already completed the activity to check their answers with a partner.

- ❑ Go around the room and check to see if students have found the answers.

- ❑ Call on two students to read their answers. Ask if the other students agree. Confirm the answers.

ANSWER KEY

From Paragraph B: The city of Curitiba, Brazil, proves that it's possible for even a city in a developing country to offer a good life to its residents.

From Paragraph G: Curitiba is truly, as Lewis Mumford once said of cities in general, a "symbol of the possible."

Strategy

Identifying Supporting Details

- Read this paragraph to the class or call on a student to read it.

- On the board, draw a large box on the left side and several smaller ones on the right side. Connect them with lines like the ones on page 30.

- Write *Main Idea* in the large box and *Details* in each of the smaller ones.

- Tell the students that this type of graphic organizer will help them to understand a reading passage better.

Best Practice

Organizing Information

Activities such as this will teach students to organize information from a reading passage using a graphic organizer. This activity allows students to locate the information so that they can better recall it at a later date. In this case, they record the main idea and supporting details from three paragraphs in the reading passage.

7 Identifying Supporting Details

- ❏ Read the directions.

- ❏ Read the words in the first box on the left and the first box on the right.

- ❏ Tell the students they have to find three more details about "*Green Exchange*" and write them in the other three boxes.

- ❏ Check the answers together before they do the next set of boxes.

- ❏ Put students in pairs and tell them to fill in the remaining boxes about Paragraphs D and E with a partner.

- ❏ Give them a time limit of 10–15 minutes.

- ❏ Go around the room and check students' answers.

- ❏ When most of the students have finished, check the answers.

ANSWER KEY

Wording of answers may vary.

C. cleans the streets of trash
exchanges trash for fresh produce
recycles two-thirds of garbage
gives jobs to poor people

D. decreases traffic
makes commuting more pleasant
helps solve problem of air pollution

E. gives poor people jobs
helps them turn their lives around

counseling
medical care
job training

UNDERSTANDING ITALICS

- Print a word on the board in straight letters, for example, huge. Then print it in slanted letters, for example, *huge*.

- Tell students that italics mean that the letters are slanted or leaning to one side.

- Read the sentences in the box or have two students read them.

■ Tell them that they are going to look for italics in the reading passage.

8 Understanding Italics

❑ Read the directions.

❑ Tell students to work quickly.

❑ When they have finished, ask them to count the number of words or phrases they circled (5) and the number of words/phrases they underlined (3).

❑ Elicit the words from the class, one by one.

ANSWER KEY

Paragraph A	*some*	emphasis
Paragraph B	*aren't*	emphasis
Paragraph C	*Cambio Verde*	foreign
	two-thirds	emphasis
Paragraph D	*decreased*	emphasis
	before	emphasis
Paragraph E	*Fazenda da Solidaridade*	foreign
	Verde Saude	foreign

UNDERSTANDING CONTRAST

■ Call on a student to read the information in the Box.

9 Understanding Contrast

❑ Read the directions.

❑ Ask students to look back at the reading.

❑ Give them a few minutes to find the contrast and decide where it can be divided (between Paragraphs B and C). Paragraphs A and B describe the problems; the remaining paragraphs describe some of the solutions.

❑ Ask a student to read the last sentence of paragraph B and tell what the contrasting words are (problems/solutions).

Critical Thinking: Making Inferences

■ Read the directions.

■ Write these sentences on the board:

   The average income in Curitiba was only $2,000 per year.
   Many people didn't have enough money to live well.

■ Point out that in the first sentence, the information is clearly stated. In the second sentence, the idea is implied, but not clearly stated.

■ Tell the students they will look back at the reading to do the next activity.

10 Making Inferences

❑ Read the directions.

❑ Give students a time limit to do the activity (10–15 minutes).

❑ Check the answers when they have finished.

ANSWER KEY

1. S 2. I 3. S 4. S 5. I 6. S 7. I 8. S 9. I 10. S

11 Discussing the Reading

❑ Divide students into small groups from different countries or regions, if possible.

❑ Have them discuss the questions in this section. They may not know some of the answers.

❑ When they finish, do the Expansion Activity on the next page.

Best Practice

Interacting with Others

Activities such as this will encourage the students to work together to complete a project. Since there are several different areas of research, students can work individually and then share their findings with the group, enlarging their scope of learning.

 REPRODUCIBLE   **EXPANSION ACTIVITY**

- The aim of this activity is for students to do collaborative research on the topics from the discussion of the reading. They will share this information with their group and then each group will share it with the class.

- Photocopy and distribute **Black Line Master 4** "Major Cities" on page BLM4 of this Teacher's Edition.

- Tell students to choose a country and complete the sheet, looking up information on the Internet.

- When they have finished, ask them to share their findings with the class.

Sick-Building Syndrome

Before You Read

1 Making Predictions

- ❑ Ask students if they ever see any pollution outside.

- ❑ Then ask them if there is any pollution inside buildings, like houses, schools, malls, or other places.

- ❑ Tell them to look at pages 32–33, read the directions and look at the chart.

- ❑ Divide them into small groups and have them complete the chart.

- ❑ When they finish, elicit answers and write them on the board.

ANSWER KEY

Answers may vary.

Causes of Outdoor Air Pollution	Causes of Indoor Air Pollution
— *motorcycles, cars, buses, trucks, trains, ships* — *factories, industrial complexes* — *plants that produce electricity, natural gas, petroleum, or nuclear power*	— *smoking cigarettes, cigars, pipes* — *fires for cooking or heating, stoves* — *chemicals in household cleaners, paint, varnish, carpets, insulation, or other synthetic materials*

Read

2 Skimming for Main Ideas

- ❑ Read the directions.

- ❑ Have the students read the passage silently within a time limit (10–15 minutes), or have them follow along as you play the audio.

- ❑ After each paragraph, stop the audio and have the students write the topic and main idea of the paragraph.

- ❑ As an alternative, have them underline the topic and main idea as they're listening, and when the passage is finished, have them discuss their answers with a small group before they write them.

- ❑ Remind them **not** to use a dictionary during this part of the lesson.

- ❑ Start the audio.

- ❑ When the passage is finished, check the answers with the class.

ANSWER KEY

Answers may vary.

[A] Topic: Sick-building syndrome

    Main Idea: Some buildings create their own indoor air pollution.

[B] Topic: Indoor air pollution

    Main Idea: The air inside some buildings is full of pollutants . . .

[C] Topic: Types of indoor air pollution

    Main Idea: Many products give off chemicals we can't see but breathe in.

[D] Topic: How indoor air becomes polluted

    Main Idea: Some products release chemicals into the air and lack of ventilation makes the situation more serious.

[E] Topic: Solutions to sick-building syndrome

    Main Idea: Experts must determine the cause and workers must remove it.

[F] Topic: Plants as a solution

    Main Idea: Some plants remove pollutants from the air.

[G] Topic: More research is necessary

Main Idea: Plants may offer an important pollution-control system for 21st century.

After You Read

Best Practice

Cultivating Critical Thinking

Activities such as comparing answers with a partner encourage students to listen to and learn from others. By not depending completely on the teacher to supply all the answers, students become more independent and learn to engage in critical thinking.

3 Checking Your Answers

❑ When the passage is finished, put students into pairs or small groups to check their answers from Activity 2.

❑ Go around and answer questions and check answers.

❑ If there is time, students can go to the board and write the **Topic** and **Main Idea** so the class can check all together.

4 Understanding Pronoun Reference

❑ Read the directions.

❑ Tell students to continue working in small groups to find the referents to the pronouns.

❑ When they are finished, check the answers.

ANSWER KEY

1. teachers and students 2. people 3. chemicals
4. sources 5. solutions 6. workers 7. plants

5 Discussing the Reading

❑ Read the directions.

❑ Tell students to continue working in small groups to discuss the answers to the questions.

❑ Ask students to share answers with the class.

Responding in Writing

6 Summarizing

❑ Remind students of the lesson on Summarizing from Chapter 1. Ask them these questions:

What do summaries contain? (main idea and important details)

Should they be copied from the paragraph? (No, they should be in writer's own words.)

Should they be as long as the original paragraph? (No, they should be shorter.)

❑ Read the directions.

❑ Divide the class into 3 sections. Assign one of the paragraphs (C, D, or E) from Part 1 on page 28 to each section.

❑ Have them read their paragraph again, and then tell them to look at the graphic organizer on pages 30–31 where the main idea and important details have already been written.

❑ Tell them to write the summary from the graphic organizer.

❑ Go around the room and check the students' work.

❑ If they finish early, they can read the summary of another student in the same section.

❑ If there is time, ask one student from each section to write his or her summary on the board and go over them with the class.

7 **Writing Your Own Ideas**

Best Practice

Scaffolding Instruction

Activities such as developing a model with students enable them to be more successful when they work independently. This activity uses the students' prior knowledge of the reading as a scaffold. With the teachers' guidance, the students are able to contribute to the summary on the board. Then they are better equipped to write a summary by themselves.

❑ Tell students to choose one of the topics for homework.

❑ In class have the students think about and write the main idea of their paragraph and then complete the paragraph at home.

Talk it Over

8 **Interviewing**

 EXPANSION ACTIVITY

■ The aim of this activity is for students to gather opinions and predictions from others while interacting in English. They will share this information with the class when they are finished.

■ Photocopy and distribute **Black Line Master 5** "City Life In The Future" on page BLM5 of this Teacher's Edition.

■ Model the activity. Call on a student and say *"Hello. My name is . . . , and I'm interviewing people for a class assignment. Can you tell me your opinion about city life? Will it be better or worse than it is today? Can you tell me two reasons why? Can you make predictions about how city life will be different in the future?*

■ Point out that they should conduct these interviews in English, if possible. They should also write the person's answers on the paper.

■ Give students a few days to complete this assignment.

■ When it is finished, elicit answers from students in a large group format. Write some of the reasons and predictions on the board.

1 Focusing on Words from the Academic Word List

- ❏ Read the directions.
- ❏ Give students a time limit (10–15 minutes).
- ❏ Tell students to check their answers with a partner if they finish quickly.
- ❏ Ask how many got all correct, one wrong, two wrong, and so on.

ANSWER KEY

1. predict 2. global 3. transportation 4. access
5. residents 6. Under 7. established 8. focus
9. environment 10. income 11. creative

Strategy

Scanning

- ■ Read the Strategy Box together.

Strategy

Understanding Parts of Speech

- ■ Write the sentence from the **Example** on the board along with the following sentence and point out the parts of speech:

  noun
  Cities around the <u>globe</u> need to find solutions to similar problems, so city

  adjective
  planners sometimes meet at a <u>global</u> conference. They discuss issues that

  adverb
  affect them <u>globally</u>.

- ■ Then tell the students to look at page 40. Read the directions in the box.

- ■ Ask a student to read the sentences on the board. Explain the parts of speech in the sentences.

2 Understanding Parts of Speech

- ❏ Tell the students to look at the chart in the following section. Read the directions.
- ❏ After the students have completed the chart, play the audio as students check their answers.

ANSWER KEY

1. beautiful 2. create 3. crowd 4. differ
5. difficulty 6. efficiently 7. polluted 8. prediction
9. safe 10. solution 11. worse

- ❏ Read the directions of the next section. Students can work individually or in pairs.

ANSWER KEY

1. solution (n) / solve (v) 2. pollution (n) / pollutants (n) 3. crowds (n) / crowded (adj)
4. safe (adj) / safely (adv) / safety (n) 5. beautiful (adj) / beautify (v) 6. predict (v) / worse (adj) / predictions (n) / worsen (v) 7. differ (v) / difference (n) / differently (adv) / different (adj)
8. efficient (adj) / efficiently (adv)

LOOKING UP PARTS OF SPEECH

- ■ Read the directions.
- ■ On the board, write a few prepositions (by, at, in) and conjunctions (and, but, or) so that students know what they are.
- ■ Write these sentences on the board and elicit the parts of speech for the underlined words from the students:

noun

A: The <u>reason</u> he was late is that the subway wasn't running.

    verb   *conjunction*   *adverb*

So he <u>had to walk</u> to class, <u>but</u> he walked as <u>quickly</u> as possible.

    adjective

B: That sounds <u>reasonable</u>. It's about a mile from his

    preposition

house <u>to</u> the university.

3   Looking up Parts of Speech

❑   Tell the students that this activity will be a contest.

❑   Instruct them to look up the words in their dictionaries. If students have both electronic and paperback dictionaries, divide them into two groups. The students who finish first in each group are the winners.

❑   Check the answers of the winners to make sure they put both possible parts of speech for answers 2, 3, 4, 6, 8, 9, 11, 14, and 15.

❑   Have them read their answers to the class.

ANSWER KEY

1. adj 2. n/v 3. n/v 4. n/adj 5. adj 6. n/v 7. n
8. n/v 9. n/v 10. n 11. n/v 12. adv 13. n
14. n/adj 15. n/v

4   Searching the Internet

Best Practice

Making Use of Academic Content

Activities such as this prepare the students for academic research. By looking up articles in online newspapers and taking notes on main ideas and details, they will become more familiar with the process of note-taking from primary sources and better prepared for academic work.

❑   Take the students to the computer lab or have them go after class to do this assignment with **Black Line Master 6**.

 EXPANSION ACTIVITY

■   The aim of this activity is for students to find an online newspaper in English from a different country and read an article. They will look up this information with a partner and then share their article with the class.

■   Photocopy and distribute **Black Line Master 6** "English–Language Newspapers" on page BLM6 of this Teacher's Edition.

■   Have the students work in pairs and let them choose (or assign them) a country.

■   They can use Google or <u>www. onlinenewspapers.com</u> to find a newspaper.

■   Tell students to find an article about the capital city and write some main ideas and details from the article.

■   Give students a few days to complete this assignment.

■   When it is finished, ask students to report their findings to the class.

GETTING MEANING OF VOCABULARY FROM CONTEXT

- Write these terms on the board:

  Close in meaning correct—not correct

  Correct part of speech—wrong meaning

  Wrong answer

  Wrong part of speech

- Read or explain the instructions in the Strategy Box to the students and refer to the terms on the board.

1 Practice

- ❑ Read the directions and have the students complete the activity.

- ❑ As you check the answers, ask students why the other answers are not correct. Refer to the terms on board.

ANSWER KEY

1. c/b 2. d 3. c 4. d

Self-Assessment Log

- ❑ Read the directions aloud and have students check vocabulary they learned in the chapter and are prepared to use.

- ❑ Have students check the strategies practiced in the chapter (or the degree to which they learned them). They have actually used all these strategies in Chapter 2.

- ❑ Put students in small groups. Ask students to find the information or an activity related to each strategy in the group.

- ❑ Tell students to find definitions in the chapter for any words they did not check.

Best Practice

Activating Prior Knowledge

Activities such as this, help students make text-to-text connections. They have previewed the vocabulary, read it in the passage, and practiced it in the activities. Doing a dictation will help the students to use the words in a slightly different context and test their knowledge. It will also allow the teacher to see if the students have actually learned the words from the chapter and incorporated them into their lexicon.

EXPANSION ACTIVITY

- The aim of this activity is for students to practice writing words from the reading passage in this chapter in sentences.

- Tell the students to study the vocabulary for a few minutes for a dictation.

- Have them take out a piece of paper.

- Dictate these sentences to them. The underlined words are from the list:

  1. Urban dwellers in developing countries have to solve many environmental problems.

  2. Often, their leaders do not have access to a lot of money, so they have to be creative and make a list of priorities.

  3. When they establish which problems they will work on, they focus on them and develop efficient methods for solving them.

  4. Generally, they involve mass transit, trash recycling, crowded living, and agricultural operations.

  5. Although the cities are not affluent, some leaders produce results by predicting that with the help of the public, these problems can be solved.

- When the students have finished, collect the papers and check them.

- For variety, have them write the sentences on the board and check their own papers.

3

Business and Money

In this chapter, students will read about different aspects of business and money, from people who cannot afford to buy anything to people who buy too much. In the first reading, they will learn about microlending and two important leaders in this movement: Mohammad Yunus from Bangladesh and Anne Firth Murray from the United States. Both these leaders saw that the only way to eradicate poverty was to give the poor a chance to support themselves through small businesses and to develop solutions to their own problems. In the second reading, students will learn about the psychology of consumerism, or the way advertisers convince us to buy things we don't need. By targeting our dissatisfaction or fear, marketing experts are better able to sell us products that may be unnecessary or even dangerous.

Chapter Opener

- ❑ Direct students' attention to the photo on page 47 of the Student Book and ask questions: *What do you see? Where do you think this is? What are the people doing? What country do you think this is?*

- ❑ Read the quotation by Butterworth and ask students what it means.

- ❑ Put two words on the board: *Prosperity* and *Poverty*

- ❑ Put students in pairs to find several words or phrases to put under each word.

- ❑ Call on students to share their words or phrases with the class.

- ❑ Check students' comprehension of the words: *Prosperity* and *Poverty*.

❝ Prosperity is a way of living and thinking, and not just money or things. Poverty is a way of living and thinking, and not just a lack of money or things. ❞

—Eric Butterworth
Scholar, author of *Spiritual Economics* (1916–2003)

Chapter Overview

Reading Selections

Banking on Poor Women

Consumerism and the Human Brain

Reading Skills and Strategies

Previewing the topic and vocabulary

Identifying the main idea and details

Understanding conclusions

Skimming for the topic and the main ideas

Critical Thinking Skills

Identifying problems and solutions

Organizing ideas using a graphic organizer

Comparing and contrasting

Making inferences

Understanding irony

Analyzing advertisements

Summarizing a paragraph

Vocabulary Building

Getting meaning from context (*e.g.* and *i.e.*)

Using parts of speech to understand vocabulary

Using suffixes to identify parts of speech

Recognizing synonyms

Focusing on the Academic Word List

Language Skills

Understanding pronoun reference

Discussing social problems and solutions

Analyzing advertisements

Writing a paragraph

Focus on Testing TOEFL® IBT

Focusing on implications and inferences

Vocabulary

Nouns		Verbs	Adjectives	Expressions
access*	grants*	consume*	addicted to	in a similar way
capacity*	items	died of (something)	(something)	peer pressure
character	logic*	funding*	anonymous	social ills
common knowledge	marketers	influence	identical*	take up space
consumer*	microlending	inform	social	
dental floss	poverty	lift	subsidiary*	
dental hygiene	requirement*	offend	worthless	
dissatisfaction with	sport utility vehicle	persuade (someone) to		
(something)	success	(do something)		
economy*	violence	plow		
eradication		take advantage of		
fear of (something)		(something)		
fund*		targeting*		

*These words are from the Academic Word List. For more information on this list,
see www.vuw.ac.nz/lals/research/awl.

Banking on Poor Women

Before You Read

1 Previewing the Topic

❑ Put students in pairs and have them look at the photos.

❑ Have students read the questions on pages 48–49 and discuss the answers with a partner.

❑ Call on students to share their answers with the class.

❑ Write some of the problems and solutions on the board and discuss them with the class.

2 Thinking Ahead

❑ Read the quotations to the students.

❑ Ask the students to restate them and write a restatement on the board for each one.

❑ Ask the class which ones they agree or disagree with and why.

3 Previewing Vocabulary

❑ Read the directions to the students.

❑ Have them put a check (✓) next to the words they know.

❑ Tell them to put the stress on words of more than one syllable as they listen to the audio.

❑ Write these words on the board as examples: *capa'city, pov'erty, anon'ymous*.

❑ Remind them **not** to use a dictionary during this part of the lesson.

❑ Start the audio.

ANSWER KEY

Nouns	Verbs
capa'city	fun'ding
cha'racter	lift
colla'teral	plow
eradica'tion	took (take) the ini'tiative
fund	**Adjectives**
grants	ano'nymous
li'teracy	subsi'diary
microlen'ding	worth'less
po'verty	**Expressions**
require'ment	so'cial ills
	peer' pressure

Strategy

Getting Meaning from Context

■ On the board, put the phrase *Clues to Meaning*. Under it, write the following abbreviations and examples:
  1. *e.g. = for example*
  2. *i.e. = that is; in other words*

■ *She traveled through several countries in Latin America—e.g., Argentina, Bolivia, and Chile.*

■ *She worked as a photojournalist; i.e., she took pictures and wrote stories about the people she met.*

■ Tell students to look for these new clues to meaning when they see words or phrases they don't understand. These clues will help them understand new words and phrases.

4 Getting Meaning from Context

❑ Read the directions and have students work on the activity individually.

ANSWER KEY

1. entrepreneurs = people who own and run their own small businesses
2. peer pressure = group members make sure that each person pays back his or her loan
3. social ills = violence and lack of education

Strategy

Recognizing Similar Meanings but Different Parts of Speech

■ Write the example from the **Strategy Box** on the board.

■ Above **poverty**, write *noun*, and above **poor**, write *adjective*.

■ Read the explanation to the students.

■ Write another example on the board: *There may be social ills when many people in a society have no money to buy necessities*.

■ Above **social**, write *adjective*, and above **society**, write *noun*.

■ Repeat the explanation to the students.

5 Recognizing Synonyms

❑ Read the directions.

❑ Ask a student to read the sentence.

❑ Call on different students to give the answers.

ANSWER KEY

1. n 2. is honest 3. n 4. is able to run her business

Strategy

Using Parts of Speech to Understand Vocabulary

■ Write the example sentence in the **Strategy Box** on the board.

■ Read the first part of the explanation to the students.

■ Ask them what part of speech **approve** is and write *verb* above it.

■ Ask them what they think it means and write their answers on the board (*agree*, *say OK about*, *sign*).

■ Read the last part of the explanation.

6 Using Parts of Speech to Understand Vocabulary

❑ Read the directions.

❑ Remind students **not** to use a dictionary during this part of the lesson.

❑ Go around the room and help students if necessary.

ANSWER KEY

Answers may vary.

1. lift	v.	bring, carry
2. eradication	n.	elimination, removal
3. subsidiary	adj.	side, minor
4. fund	n.	account, group, money
grant	n.	not loans, money given
5. plow	v.	put, return

7 Reading an Article

❑ Write *"How can banks help poor women to change their lives?"* on the board and ask students to think about this question as they are reading.

❏ Have the students read the passage silently within a time limit (10–15 minutes), or have them follow along as you play the audio.

❏ Tell them to underline any words or phrases that are new or that they don't understand.

❏ Remind them **not** to use a dictionary during this part of the lesson.

❏ Start the audio.

After You Read

Strategy

Organizing Ideas Using a Venn Diagram

■ Tell students to look at the **Strategy Box**.

■ Read the explanation to the students.

■ Draw a set of circles on the board (a Venn diagram). Draw a simple car and a motorcycle in the circles.

■ Elicit similarities from the students and write the words in the center. Use prompts such as *They both have/are* . . . Students may give answers like *transportation, wheels, seats, engine, gas, fast,* and so on.

■ Elicit the differences and write the words on the right or left. Students may give answers like *large, 4 wheels, big engine, 4 seats, expensive* for the car, and *small, 2 wheels, small engine, 2 seats, cheap* for the motorcycle.

■ Tell the students that a Venn diagram is a graphic organizer that they can use when they read. It will help them remember similarities and differences between two or more concepts in a reading.

■ Now look at the Venn diagram with the oranges and bananas.

■ Ask a student to read the words in the center. Ask other students to read the words on the right and left.

■ Left (yellow color, long, curved shape); right (orange color, circular shape).

■ Ask the students what the two fruits have in common. The students should give you the answers from the center of the Venn diagram—(fruit, sweet).

REPRODUCIBLE   EXPANSION ACTIVITY

■ The aim of this activity is for students to practice using Venn diagrams to differentiate between two categories. They will choose two sets of things and figure out similarities and differences. Then they will share their answers with a partner.

■ Photocopy and distribute **Black Line Master 7** "Venn Diagrams" on page BLM7 of this Teacher's Edition.

■ Write a few suggestions on the board: *two people in your family, two cities, two sports, two majors, two types of food,* and so on. Tell them to label their diagrams. Remind them they need to complete two sets of Venn diagrams.

■ Have the students work individually at first. When they finish, tell them to share their diagrams with a partner. Then tell them to switch and share their diagrams with another partner.

8 Organizing Ideas Using a Venn Diagram

❏ Read the directions.

❏ Give the students a few minutes to find the similarities and differences between the **Grameen Bank** and the **Global Fund for Women**.

❏ Go around the room and check to see if students have found the answers.

❏ Have the students check their work with a partner if they finish early.

❏ Draw two intersecting circles on the board (a Venn diagram) and ask three students to go to the board. One will write the similarities and the other two will write the differences.

❏ When they finish, ask if the other students agree. Discuss the answers.

ANSWER KEY

Grameen Bank

lends money
borrowing groups
$33 million
3.7 million borrowers
94% women
98% repayment rate

character
capacity
helps women

Global Fund for Women

gives grants
solutions to social ills
$37 million
2,500 women's groups
100% women
no repayment necessary

9 Checking Comprehension: Identifying Details

❏ Put students in small groups.

❏ Have them answer the questions together, with each group writing its answers on one piece of paper.

❏ Tell them they can use the Venn diagram or ask others in their group, but they can't look back at the reading for the answers.

❏ Ask them to share their answers with the class.

ANSWER KEY
Answers may vary.

1. To borrow money from Grameen Bank, women must have character and capacity and join a borrowing group. It isn't necessary to have collateral.

2. The bank lends to women because men usually spend money on themselves, but women spend money on the business. It doesn't lend to people in urban areas because borrowers in cities do not always repay the loans. Because of peer pressure, microlending is more effective in small villages, where everyone knows everyone else.

3. While the primary effect is the eradication of poverty, the subsidiary effect is the change in the social status of women. They receive more respect because they have more money and more capacity for business.

4. Some of the social ills associated with poverty are violence against women, lack of health care, and lack of education.

10 Critical Thinking: Making Inferences

❏ Read the directions to the students.

❏ Ask a student to read the information from paragraph E.

❏ Elicit ways in which the students think a "woman receives more respect."

❏ Write some of them on the board. Students may say:
Her husband is kind to her.
He helps her with the business.
Her neighbors buy things from her.
Her children help her at home.
She buys things that her family needs.
The people at the bank welcome her.
She sends her children to school.
The teachers talk to her about her children.
The villagers talk to her about her business.

She feels more important at home and in the village.

❑ Write the word **Inferences** above the list.

❑ Tell students that although these sentences are actually not in the reading, we can **infer** them from the reading.

11 **Discussing the Reading**

❑ Read the directions to the students.

❑ Put students in small groups.

❑ Have them talk about the answers.

❑ Ask them to share their answers with the class.

ANSWER KEY

(Answers will vary.)

1. Some banks require collateral like a car, a house, and a steady job. They may require a credit history, proving you have paid back loans in the past.

2. They may join a credit union, which is like a bank, but the interest is usually lower.

3. There might be crime, poverty, pollution, unemployment, corrupt politicians, and so forth. Political parties or other groups sometimes try to solve these problems.

12 **Talk It Over: Understanding Irony**

❑ Direct the students' attention to the cartoon.

❑ Have two students read the parts of the rich man and poor man.

❑ Ask them what they think the cartoon is expressing and if they agree with it.

❑ They may have different opinions about it.

❑ Read the definition of *irony* in the direction line.

Consumerism and the Human Brain

Before You Read

Strategy

Previewing the Topic

- Read the explanation to the students.

1   Previewing the Topic

- ❏ Read the directions to the students.
- ❏ Put the students in pairs.
- ❏ Tell them to answer the questions.
- ❏ Have them share their answers with the class.

Read

2   Identifying the Topic and Main Idea

- ❏ Read the directions.
- ❏ Have the students read the passage silently within a time limit (10–15 minutes), or have them follow along as you play the audio.
- ❏ After each paragraph, stop the audio and have the students write the topic and main idea of the paragraph.
- ❏ Or have them underline the topic and main idea as they're listening, and when the passage is finished, have them discuss their answers with a small group before they write them.
- ❏ Remind them **not** to use a dictionary during this part of the lesson.
- ❏ Start the audio.

ANSWER KEY

Answers may vary.

[A] Topic: Consumerism

Main Idea: We buy products based on marketers' successful use of psychology.

[B] Topic: Human fears

Main Idea: Our fear of offending people is greater than logic.

[C] Topic: Need for good self-image

Main Idea: Our need for a good self-image leads us to irrational decisions about products.

[D] Topic: Identical products

Main Idea: Even though products are the same, people choose one based on sensory information.

[E] Topic: Self-fulfilling prophecy

Main Idea: When we buy products, we believe what advertisers say about them, and it comes true.

[F] Topic: Making choices

Main Idea: We may not make choices independently; marketers may make them for us.

After You Read

3   Identifying the Topic and Main Idea

- ❏ Read the directions.
- ❏ Put students in pairs.
- ❏ Go around the room and answer questions.

4   Understanding Pronoun Reference

- ❏ Read the directions to the students.

ANSWER KEY

1. advertisers and marketers 2. dentists 3. men
4. a product 5. Dr. Alan Hirsch 6. consumers

Content Notes

- In the United States, there are several organizations that monitor the value and safety of products and evaluate the claims advertisers make about them. They also act as advocates for consumers and defend their rights. Two of these organizations are discussed below.

- The **Consumers Union** was an organization founded in 1936 with the mission of protecting consumers from the false claims of advertisers and the dangers of unsafe products. It began publishing a magazine that is now called **Consumer Reports**, which is still published today. There is also a website of the same name that gives ratings and recommendations on the following categories of products: cars, appliances, electronics and computers, home and garden, health and fitness, personal finance, babies and kids, travel, and food. Millions of people subscribe to the magazine or website to get the latest information on consumer products.

- **California Certified Organic Farmers** (CCOF) is an organization founded in 1973 to help farmers who wanted to use organic (not synthetic) products to produce food. This included fertilizers and pesticides for plants and food and medicine for animals. Today, the CCOF label is recognized and trusted by people who buy organic meat, vegetables, fruit, and packaged food. Products cannot be labeled "Certified Organic" unless they pass inspection by CCOF. Other organizations, like the **Organic Consumers Association**, monitor local and national regulations on the production and labeling and of food and personal products.

 EXPANSION ACTIVITY

REPRODUCIBLE

- The aim of this activity is for students to do collaborative research on a topic from the reading. They will share this information with their group, and then each group will share it with the class.

- Photocopy and distribute **Black Line Master 8** "Consumer Organizations In My Country" on page BLM8 of this Teacher's Edition.

- Tell students to complete the sheet in pairs, looking up information on the Internet. Make sure each pair chooses a different organization to research.

- When they have finished, ask them to share their findings with the class.

5 Discussing the Reading

- ❏ Read the directions.
- ❏ Have students do Steps 1 and 2 individually.
- ❏ When they finish, divide them into groups of males and females to share their lists and answers for Step 3.
- ❏ When they finish, have a class discussion about the answers.
- ❏ Ask students if they noticed any differences in the answers given by males and females.
- ❏ If there are differences, draw a Venn diagram on the board with two circles and elicit the similarities and differences, writing them on the board.

Responding in Writing

6 Summarizing

❏ Read the directions.

❏ Remind students of the lesson on Summarizing from Chapter 1. Ask them these questions:

> *What do summaries contain?* (Topic, Main idea and important details.)

> *Should they be copied from the paragraph?* (No, they should be in writer's own words.)

> *Should they be as long as the original paragraph?* (No, they should be shorter.)

❏ Assign students to a paragraph or let them choose one.

❏ Tell students to sit in small groups and compose a summary together, with each student writing on a separate paper.

❏ Have a student from each group write his or her paragraph on the board. Correct any errors.

7 Responding in Writing

❏ Assign the paragraph in this section for homework, allowing each student to choose a topic.

❏ Tell students to write the main idea on the last line in the directions for this activity.

❏ When students bring their homework in, before you collect it, tell them to exchange papers and read their partner's paragraph.

❏ Ask them to write the main idea of the summary they have just read under the paragraph.

❏ When students get their papers back, have them compare their main idea with the one their partners wrote.

❏ Collect the papers and correct.

Talk it Over

8 Discussing Advertisements

 EXPANSION ACTIVITY

■ The aim of this activity is for students to do collaborative research on a topic from the reading. They will share this information with their group and then each group will share it with the class.

■ Photocopy and distribute **Black Line Master 9** "Analyzing Advertisements" on page BLM9 of this Teacher's Edition.

■ Let each group choose a different product and find several advertisements for *toothpaste, cars, laundry detergent,* or *cigarettes.* If there are more than 4 groups, let them choose another product.

■ Tell students to answer the questions about their advertisement and write a short paragraph about what kind of psychology the advertisers are using.

■ When they have finished, have them share their findings with the class.

1 **Recognizing Word Meanings**

❑ Read the directions.

❑ Have students do the activity quickly without using a dictionary.

ANSWER KEY

1. d 2. a 3. b 4. e 5. c

2 **Focusing on Words from the Academic Word List**

❑ Read the directions.

❑ Have students do the activity quickly without using a dictionary.

❑ For variety, play the audio (first two paragraphs) and do the activity as a dictation.

❑ Have students check the answers on page 58 of the Student Book.

ANSWER KEY

1. consumers 2. consume 3. economy 4. access
5. items 6. identical 7. consume 8. targeting
9. logic

UNDERSTANDING PARTS OF SPEECH: SUFFIXES

■ Read the paragraph to the class or call on a student to read it.

■ On the board, write *Nouns* on the left side and *Adjectives* on the right side.

■ Write *actor*, *artist*, and *presentation* under *Nouns*.

■ Elicit the adjective form of these words (*active*, *artistic*, and *presentable*) and write them under *Adjectives*.

■ Underline the suffixes.

■ Tell students that recognizing suffixes will help them identify parts of speech, which will help them figure out the meaning of new words.

3 **Understanding Parts of Speech: Suffixes**

❑ Read the directions.

❑ Have students do the activity.

❑ Check the answers.

ANSWER KEY

1. adj 2. n 3. adj 4. n 5. n 6. n 7. adj 8. adj 9. n
10. n 11. adj 12. n 13. n 14. n 15. n 16. n
17. n 18. n 19. adj 20. adj 21. n 22. n 23. n
24. adj 25. n 26. adj 27. n 28. adj 29. n 30. n/
adj 31. adj 32. adj 33. n

4 **Understanding Parts of Speech: Changing the Suffix**

❑ Read the directions.

❑ Have students do the activity.

❑ Check the answers.

ANSWER KEY

1. Marketers/consumers 2. violent/offensive
3. information/influence 4. successful/society

Strategy

Paying Attention to Phrases

- Write the phrases in the **Strategy Box** on the board, marking the stress.

- Read the directions.

- Have students repeat the phrases after you.

- Have them repeat them by themselves.

Noun Phrases	**Verb Phrases**
greater ac'cess	spend mon'ey
access to informa'tion	educate people to spend wise'ly

Prepositional Phrases	**Infinitive Phrases**
in a sim'ilar way	to save mon'ey
with exciting lives'	to buy Brand X'

5 Paying Attention to Phrases

- ❑ Read the directions.

- ❑ Have students take turns reading one sentence each, saying what kind of phrase it is.

- ❑ Then say the phrases and have the students repeat them after you.

ANSWER KEY

    1. prep.   2. noun   3. prep.

For many people, there seems to be no escape from poverty; in other words, they are poor, and they

    4. verb   5. prep.   6. noun

have no hope that this will ever change. In addition, they have the social problems of poverty.

      7. verb   8. noun   9. verb   10. prep.

Imagine this situation: a poor woman has an idea for a small business to lift herself and her family

    11. prep.   12. noun   13. inf.   14. prep.   15. inf.

out of poverty. She needs a little money to begin this business. She goes to a bank to borrow the money,

                  16. prep.   17. verb

and the banker interviews her. At this bank, as at most banks, the borrower must meet three necessary

                          18. inf.   19. prep.

conditions: character, capacity, and collateral. That is, if this woman wants to borrow money from the bank,

                20. verb   21. inf.

she must show that she (1) is honest (has character), (2) is able to run her business (has capacity), and

    22. verb

(3) owns a house, land, or something valuable (has collateral) for the bank to take if she can't

    23. verb   24. verb

pay back the money. So what happens to the woman? The bank won't lend her the money because she

              25. prep.

doesn't have any collateral. In such a situation, there seems to be no way for the woman

    26. inf.

to break the cycle of poverty.

6 Noticing Words in Phrases

- ❏ Read the directions.

- ❏ Have students do the activity in pairs. Tell them to try to do it *before* reading the paragraphs.

- ❏ Tell students to check the answers themselves by reading the paragraphs.

ANSWER KEY

[A] 1. to 2. with 3. to 4. dental 5. dental 6. of

[B] 7. in 8. take/of 9. common 10. to 11. of

[C] 12. utility 13. up 14. out of

7 Searching the Internet

Best Practice

Organizing Information

Activities such as this will teach students to organize information from a Web page using a graphic organizer. This activity allows students to locate information so that they can better recall it at a later date. In this case, they look up the information on the Internet and take notes as they read.

ANSWER KEY

Organization	Question	Answer (Answers may vary.)
Grameen Bank	What types of businesses do Grameen borrowers have?	Making shoes, dairy products; selling clothing, food, plants, produce, etc.
Global Fund for Women	What is one program that the Global Fund is currently supporting?	Increasing access to education, fostering social change, expanding civic and political participation, etc.
Seikatsu Club	What are some of the club's principles on safety, health, and the environment?	Pursuit of safety for consumer materials, reduction of harmful substances, sustainable use of natural resources, etc.

TOEFL® IBT

IMPLICATIONS AND INFERENCES

- Write these terms on the board:

  Imply – communicate indirectly (not directly)

    – "The speaker implies that . . ."

    – "The author implies that . . ."

    – "Paragraph 4 implies that . . ."

  Infer – understand indirectly (not directly)

    – "The listener could infer that . . ."

    – "The reader might infer that . . ."

    – "It can be inferred from paragraph 4 that . . ."

- Read or explain the instructions to the students and refer to the terms on the board.

1　Practice

❑ Have students do the activity.

❑ As you check the answers, ask students why some of the answers are not correct. Refer to the terms on board.

ANSWER KEY

1. ✓　2. <u>infers</u> (should be implies)　3. ✓　4. F
5. <u>infers</u> (should be implies)　6. ✓　7. F　8. ✓　9. ✓
10. <u>imply</u> (should be infer)

Self-Assessment Log

❑ Read the directions aloud and have students check vocabulary they learned in the chapter and are prepared to use.

❑ Have students check the strategies practiced in the chapter (or the degree to which they learned them). They have actually used all these strategies in Chapter 3.

❑ Put students in small groups. Ask students to find the information or an activity related to each strategy in the group.

❑ Tell students to find definitions in the chapter for any words they did not check.

Best Practice

Activating Prior Knowledge

Activities such as these help students make text-to-text connections. They have previewed the vocabulary, read it in the passage, and practiced it in the activities. Making up sentences will help the students to use the words in a slightly different context and expand their knowledge. It will also allow the teacher to see if the students have actually learned the words from the chapter.

EXPANSION ACTIVITY

- The aim of this activity is for students to practice writing words in sentences from the **Academic Word List**.

- Tell the students to look at the vocabulary list on page 69 and make up 10 sentences, using as many words as possible.

- Have them take out a piece of paper and begin writing. Give them 10 minutes to complete the activity.

- When they have finished, collect the papers and check them. Tell them you will give a prize to the student who used the most words correctly.

- For variety, have each student write one sentence on the board containing as many words as possible from the list.

4

Jobs and Professions

In this chapter, students will read about how work life is changing because of globalization and technology; workers change careers several times in their lives. Some will work at home instead of at a job site, and some are even addicted to work. Then students will read about how people decide what they want to do with their life and how they acquire the necessary skills. If they are not sure, they can consult a career counselor or join a support group. They can also look for jobs on the Internet, either responding to a company's postings or putting their own curricula vitae online. Finally, students will read Peter Drucker's predictions about the rise of two classes in a post-capitalist society, in which some workers will use knowledge as the basis for production and innovation while others will provide services for them, possibly creating a social divide between these two classes.

Chapter Opener

❏ Direct students' attention to the photo on page 71 of the Student Book and ask questions: *What do you see? Where do you think this is? What are the people doing? What country do you think this is?*

❏ Read the quotation and ask students what it means.

❏ Put two phrases on the board: *Lifetime Job* and *Job Change*.

❏ Put students in pairs to discuss positive and negative aspects of these situations.

❏ Call on students to share their ideas with the class.

❝ Every job is a self-portrait of the person who does it. **❞**

—Unknown

Chapter Overview

Reading Selections

Changing Career Trends

Looking for Work in the 21st Century

Reading Skills and Strategies

Previewing the topic and vocabulary

Getting meaning from context

Previewing a reading

Identifying the main idea

Identifying important details

Skimming for the topic and the main ideas

Critical Thinking Skills

Identifying cause and effect

Organizing cause and effect using a graphic organizer

Summarizing a paragraph

Understanding proverbs and quotations

Vocabulary Building

Using the prefix *over-*

Focusing on the Academic Word List

Understanding adjective and noun phrases

Understanding and creating compound words

Language Skills

Understanding pronoun reference

Discussing proverbs and quotations

Identifying challenges and changes within today's work world

Writing a paragraph

Focus on Testing

Increasing reading speed

Vocabulary

Nouns		Verbs	Adjectives
background	livelihood	distract	flexible*
career counselors	manufacturing jobs	keep up with	leisure
cell phones	old-fashioned	overwork	online
classified ads	outsourcing	upgrade	passionate
drawback	personnel office	varies (vary)*	rigid*
dream job	posts		secure*
employment agency	self-confidence		temporary*
globalization*	technology* field		worldwide
job hopping	telecommuting		
job hunting	ulcers		
job opening	workaholism		
job security	workforce		

*These words are from the Academic Word List. For more information on this list, see www.vuw.ac.nz/lals/research/awl.

Changing Career Trends

Before You Read

1   Previewing the Topic

- ❏ Put students in pairs or small groups and have them look at the photos.

- ❏ Have students read the questions on page 72 and discuss the answers with a partner.

- ❏ Call on students to share their answers with the class.

- ❏ Write some of the changes on the board and discuss them with the class.

2   Previewing Vocabulary

- ❏ Read the directions to the students.

- ❏ Have them put a check (✓) next to the words they know.

- ❏ Tell them to put the stress on words of more than one syllable as they listen to the audio program.

- ❏ Write these words on the board as examples: *globaliza'tion, out'sourcing, keep up' with*.

- ❏ Remind them **not** to use a dictionary during this part of the lesson.

- ❏ Start the audio.

ANSWER KEY

Nouns	plea'sure	upgrade
career' counselors	posts	va'ries (vary)
cell' phones	self-con'fidence	**Adjectives**
construc'tion	stress	flex'ible
draw'back	telecommu'ting	lei'sure
globaliza'tion	ul'cers	pass'ionate
iden'tity	work'aholism	ri'gid
job' hopping	work'force	secure'
job secu'rity	**Verbs**	tem'porary
live'lihood	distract'	world'wide
manufac'turing jobs	keep up' with	**Expression**
out'sourcing	overwork	on the move'

3   Getting Meaning from Context

- ❏ Read the directions.

- ❏ Ask a student to read the first sentence.

- ❏ Call on different students to give possible answers.

- ❏ If necessary, repeat the process.

- ❏ Tell students to continue on their own.

ANSWER KEY

Answers may vary.

1. livelihood = work, job, profession
2. posts = positions, jobs
3. secure = permanent, safe
4. self-confidence = belief in their own ability, self-assurance
5. upgrade = improve, advance
6. keep up with = continue in, maintain skills in
7. telecommuting = work at home, work via the computer, phone, fax
8. distract = take attention away
9. drawback = disadvantage, unfavorable aspect
10. leisure = free time, time away from work
11. globalization = work done all over the world, companies in different countries
12. flexible = changeable, adjusting well to change; rigid = not flexible
13. workaholism = addiction to working, unable to stop working

4   Comparing Answers

- ❏ Ask students to take turns reading the sentences and giving answers, which may vary.

- ❏ Write any difficult ones on the board if necessary and discuss them.

❏ Tell students to go back to the vocabulary chart in **Activity 2** and put a check (✓) beside the new words they have just learned.

Strategy

Previewing a Reading

▪ Write the bullet points from the **Strategy Box** on the board:

> headings——"titles" of paragraphs
> pictures——photos or images
> charts, figures, graphs, diagrams

▪ Read the contents of the **Strategy Box**.

▪ Tell students to look at the reading "Changing Career Trends" on pages 75--77.

▪ Point out the headings, the pictures, and the chart.

▪ Tell them that these will give them an idea of what the reading is about.

5 Previewing a Reading

❏ Read the directions.

❏ Ask students the questions.

❏ Call on different students to give the answers.

❏ Elicit a few questions from students and write them on the board.

Read

6 Reading an Article

❏ Write on the board: *What are some ways in which work is changing?*

❏ Have the students read the passage silently within a time limit (10–15 minutes), or have them follow along as you play the audio.

❏ Tell them to underline any words or phrases that are new or that they don't understand.

❏ Remind them **not** to use a dictionary during this part of the lesson.

❏ Start the audio.

After You Read

7 Finding the Main idea

❏ Read the directions.

❏ Have different students read each item aloud.

❏ Ask how many think the main idea is **A**, **B**, **C**, **D**, or **E**.

❏ Tell those who guessed **C** that they are correct.

❏ Go over each item and explain that **A**, **B**, **D**, and **E** are about specific topics in the reading, but **C** is the main idea of the reading as a whole.

8 Comprehension Check: Finding Important Details

❏ Read the directions.

❏ Have students work in pairs to find the statements that are true according to the reading.

❏ Check the answers.

ANSWER KEY

1.✓ 2.✓ 4.✓ 5.✓ 6.✓ 8.✓

9 Checking Vocabulary

❏ Read the directions.

❏ Have the students work individually or in pairs to find the words or expressions.

❏ Check the answers.

ANSWER KEY

1. career counselors 2. job security
3. outsourcing 4. job hopping 5. drawback

Strategy

Critical Thinking: Recognizing Cause and Effect

- Write on the board:
  causes → effects
  reasons → results

- Read the information in the **Strategy Box**, pointing to the words on the board.

10 **Critical Thinking: Recognizing Cause and Effect**

Best Practice

Organizing Information

Activities such as this will teach students to organize information from a reading using a graphic organizer. This activity helps students to recognize cause and effect so that they can better understand the reading. In this case, they look up the information and determine the relationships among the facts presented.

- ❏ Read the directions.
- ❏ Have the students work individually or in pairs to find the causes and effects.
- ❏ Check the answers.

ANSWER KEY

Cause	Effect
a decrease in manufacturing jobs	a lack of job security
employers' need to hold down costs	
employers' need to hold down costs	**more temporary jobs**
	outsourcing

well-educated workforce (in India)	
salaries are lower	outsourcing to India
educated people fluent in English	

USING THE PREFIX *OVER-*

- Write these sentences on the board:
  Some people _overwork_ and don't enjoy their job.
  Other people _overeat_ and gain weight.
  When workers are _overtired_, they can't perform well.

- Ask students to guess the meaning of the underlined words.

- Read the explanation in the box to the students.

- Ask them what part of speech _overwork_ and _overeat_ is and write *verb* above them.

- Ask them what part of speech _overtired_ is and write *adjective* above it.

- Read the explanation in the box, and tell students that the prefix *over-* can be used with verbs or adjectives.

11 **Using the Prefix *Over-***

- ❏ Read the directions.
- ❏ Check answers after students compare them.
- ❏ Point out the difference in spelling and meaning of *overdo* and *overdue*.

ANSWER KEY

1. overdo 2. overcrowded 3. overestimate
4. overdue 5. overpopulation

EXPANSION ACTIVITY

- The aim of this activity is to help students do collaborative research on the topic of cell phone use. They will share this information with a partner and then with the rest of the class.

- Read the text in the box and ask students the questions at the end.

- Photocopy and distribute **Black Line Master 10** "Cell Phone Use" on page BLM10 of this Teacher's Edition.

- Tell students to keep a log for one week, showing it to their partner every day.

- When they have finished, have each student make a pie chart from the log, using a simple computer application that generates a display from data input. Tell them to ask for help if they have difficulty.

- Ask a volunteer to gather all the logs and make a pie chart for cell phone use of women and of men in the class, and one of all the logs combined.

- Compare the pie charts to see if there are differences.

Best Practice

Interacting with Others

Activities such as this will encourage students to work together to gather data. Having to compare logs with a partner will remind them to keep track of phone use. Having to make a pie chart together will help them learn a new computer skill. This will show them that engaging in peer interaction and collaboration will help them academically.

12 Discussing the Reading

- ❑ Divide the students into groups, either from the same country or different countries.

- ❑ Tell them to choose one person to take notes and another person to share the findings with the class.

- ❑ Give them a time limit (10–15 minutes).

- ❑ When the time is up, tell them to share the findings with the class.

Looking for Work in the 21st Century

Before You Read

1 Thinking Ahead

- ❑ Read the directions.
- ❑ Put students in pairs.
- ❑ Tell them to answer the questions.
- ❑ Have them share their answers with the class.

2 Skimming for the Topic and the Main Idea

- ❑ Read the directions.
- ❑ Have the students read the passage silently within a time limit (10–15 minutes), or have them follow along as you play the audio.
- ❑ After each paragraph, stop the audio and have the students write the topic and main idea of the paragraph.
- ❑ Or have them underline the topic and main idea as they're listening, and when the passage is finished, have them discuss their answers with a small group before they write them.
- ❑ Remind them **not** to use a dictionary during this part of the lesson.
- ❑ Start the audio.

ANSWER KEY

Answers may vary.

[A] Topic: Finding a job

Main Idea: In the past, finding a job was a simple process with only a few steps.

[B] Topic: Job hunting now is more complex

Main Idea: Now you have to go through more complicated steps to find a new job.

[C] Topic: Career counselors

Main Idea: People go to career counselors, who tell them to find a job they love.

[D] Topic: Job hunting on the Internet

Main Idea: Many employers advertise jobs online, and many people apply for them.

[E] Topic: Job hunting on job boards

Main Idea: People post their résumés on the Internet, and companies can do some of the interviewing online as well.

After You Read

3 Checking Your Answers

- ❑ Read the directions.
- ❑ Put students in pairs to compare their answers.
- ❑ Go around the room and answer questions.

4 Understanding Pronoun Reference

- ❑ Read the directions
- ❑ Tell the students to work in pairs to find the referents.
- ❑ Check the answers with the class.

ANSWER KEY

1. people 2. kind of job 3. their dream job 4. job boards 5. the next step 6. job hunting

5 Discussing the Reading

- ❑ Read the directions.
- ❑ Put students into small groups.
- ❑ Have them answer the questions together.
- ❑ Ask them to share any interesting things they learned with the class.

Content Notes

- *Globalization* has many different meanings. The term is usually used to mean the current socio-economic situation in which capitalism, or the free-market economy, has spread to other countries. Goods and services are provided by people from other countries, so more profits are made.

- Most of the clothes we wear and the items we buy come from other countries. They may be designed in our country, but they are manufactured in another, where the cost of labor is lower. They are shipped and sold all over the world, and many consumers are glad that the cost of these items is lower. However, they are also upset because many factories have closed and jobs have been outsourced, leaving some people unemployed.

- The meaning of *globalization* in the **Cultural Note** on page 84 is slightly different from the above meaning. The five criteria given indicate that it means how well-connected a country is to the rest of the world via cell phones and computers, how involved the citizens are in the politics of the country, how freely other nationalities can move in and out of the country, and now how vibrant the country's economy is.

- Considering this meaning, ask the students to guess which five countries are the most *globalized*. You can put the countries they suggest on the board, and then take a vote. Or students can go to the board and "vote for" five countries by putting a check (✓) after them. When you tally the scores, you can announce the countries:

- ANSWER KEY: 1) Singapore, 2) Ireland, 3) Switzerland, 4) the United States, and 5) the Netherlands.

Making Use of Academic Content

Activities such as this prepare the students for academic research. By conducting surveys and assembling the data gathered in displays, they will become more familiar with the process and better prepared for academic work.

 EXPANSION ACTIVITY

- The aim of this activity is for students to do collaborative research on a topic in the chapter. They will share this information with their group and then with the class.

- Photocopy and distribute **Black Line Master 11** "Survey of Globalized Countries" on page BLM11 of this Teacher's Edition.

- Let each group choose a different nationality or age group to survey. Examples of age groups are 20–29, 30–39, 40–49, 50–59, and so on. Have the class agree on either nationality or age group; gender within this category can then be considered.

- Tell students to interview at least 10 people in the category (5 men and 5 women) and record their answers.

- When they are have finished, have students go to the computer lab and make a bar graph with the statistics they have collected. They can use a simple program that automatically builds the graph from the data entered.

- Have them assemble their data displays on a poster board or bulletin board and share their information with the class.

Responding in Writing

6 Summarizing

- ❑ Read the directions.

- ❑ Assign students to a topic or let them choose one.

- ❑ Tell students to sit in small groups and compose a summary together, with each student writing on a separate paper.

- ❑ Have one student from each group write the paragraph on the board. Correct any errors.

- ❑ If there is time, have the students copy the other two paragraphs from the board after they are corrected.

7 Writing Your Own Ideas

Best Practice

Scaffolding Instruction

Activities such as this, allowing students to work together, will enable them to be more successful when they work independently. This activity uses the students' prior knowledge of the reading as a scaffold. With their classmates' input, students are able to contribute to the group's summary. Later, they will be better equipped to write a summary by themselves.

- ❑ Assign the paragraph in this section for homework, allowing each student to choose a topic.

- ❑ Have each student write the main idea of their paragraph on the line in their books.

- ❑ When the students bring their homework in, before you collect it, tell students to exchange papers and read their partner's paragraph.

- ❑ Ask them to write the main idea of the summary they have just read under the paragraph.

- ❑ When students get their papers back, have them compare their main idea in their books with the one their partners wrote on the papers.

- ❑ Collect the papers and correct.

Talk It Over

8 Discussing Proverbs and Quotations

- ❑ Read the directions.

- ❑ Read the proverbs and quotations to the students and have them repeat them after you.

- ❑ Divide them into small groups to discuss the answers to the questions.

- ❑ Have them share their ideas with the class.

ANSWER KEY

"All work and no play makes Jack a dull boy." = If a person works all the time, he will be boring; he won't have anything interesting to do or say.

"Ninety percent of inspiration is perspiration." = [Similar to Thomas Edison's quotation: *"Genius is one percent inspiration and ninety percent perspiration."*] = A genius (very intelligent person) spends much more time working on her ideas than thinking about them.

"Work expands to fill up the time available." = If we have a month to do a project, it will take a month; if we have only a week, it will take only a week.

"Laziness travels so slowly that poverty soon overtakes him." = If a person is lazy, he will become poor because he doesn't earn enough money to live.

"It is neither wealth nor splendor, but tranquility and occupation, which give happiness." = Being peaceful and occupied (working) makes people happier than being rich or having a fancy lifestyle.

1 **Focusing on Words from the Academic Word List**

❑ Read the directions.

❑ Have students do the activity quickly without using a dictionary.

❑ For variety, play the audio (first half of paragraph B in "Changing Career Trends") and do the activity as a dictation.

❑ Have students check the answers on page 75 in the Student Book.

ANSWER KEY

1. varies 2. economy 3. traditionally 4. secure
5. job 6. job security 7. jobs 8. enormous
9. creating 10. temporary 11. benefits 12. areas
13. labor 14. computer

UNDERSTANDING ADJECTIVE AND NOUN PHRASES

■ On the board, write *Adjective Phrases* and *Noun Phrases*.

■ Under *Adjective Phrases*, write *part-time*, *especially interesting*, and *fastest-growing*.

■ Under *Noun Phrases*, write *city life, social sciences, self-confidence,* and *word-of-mouth*.

■ Read the explanation to the class or call on students to read it.

■ Call students' attention to the board, and elicit the parts of speech for each word in the phrase, writing the abbreviations, i.e.,such as *adj., noun,* and *adv*.

■ Tell students that recognizing adjective and noun phrases will help them figure out the meaning of new words.

---

2 **Understanding Adjective and Noun Phrases**

❑ Read the directions.

❑ Have students do the activity.

❑ Check the answers.

ANSWER KEY

1. classified/dream 2. unemployment/part/self
3. city/shopping/mass/traffic 4. career/computer
5. job/personnel

3 **Creating Adjective and Noun Phrases**

❑ Read the directions.

❑ Have students do the activity.

❑ Check the answers.

ANSWER KEY

1. d 2. a 3. h 4. e 5. b 6. g 7. c 8. f

UNDERSTANDING COMPOUND WORDS

■ Have a student read the explanation and example sentence.

■ Have students tell you the two words in each compound word.

  sales + clerk
  super + market

---

4 **Understanding Compound Words**

❑ Read the directions.

❑ Have students do the activity.

❑ Check the answers.

ANSWER KEY

1. h over/seas 2. e draw/back 3. j over/crowding
4. a grid/lock 5. i world/wide 6. b over/work
7. c work/force 8. f up/grade 9. d on/line
10. g back/ground

5 Creating Compound Words and Phrases

❑ Read the directions.

❑ Have students do the activity in small groups.

❑ Check the answers.

❑ Give a prize to the winners.

ANSWER KEY

Answers may vary.

city life	*job interview*	*public college*
city planning	*job market*	*science lab*
college exam	*life science*	*security*
college tuition	*life work*	*department*
computer lab	*network security*	*self-confidence*
high school	*office job*	*self-service*
		Web planning

6 Searching the Internet

❑ Ask students if they have ever tried to find a job on the Internet.

❑ Invite them to share their experiences with the class.

❑ Direct their attention to this section and read the directions.

❑ See Expansion Activity.

Best Practice

Cultivating Critical Thinking

Activities such as searching online job boards encourage students to look at Internet use more critically. By evaluating a website, looking at jobs, and actually applying for a position, students can become more familiar with the process and better able to choose an appropriate website in the future.

EXPANSION ACTIVITY
REPRODUCIBLE

■ The aim of this activity is for students to do collaborative research on this topic from the second reading. They will share this information with their group and then each group will share it with the class.

■ Photocopy and distribute **Black Line Master 12** "Online Job Boards" on page BLM12 of this Teacher's Edition.

■ Print out the following URLs on pieces of paper and let students (in pairs) choose one at random: www.careerbuilder.com; hotjobs.yahoo.com; jobsjobsjobs.com; www.jobster.com; www.jobweb.com; www.monster.com.

■ Tell students to go to the Computer Lab with their partners or use their own computers after class.

■ Have them look up the website and follow the directions.

■ When they have finished, have them share their findings with the class.

FASTER READING SPEED—LEFT-TO-RIGHT EYE MOVEMENT

- Read the directions and go over the **Example** activity.

- Tell students that these exercises activities are especially useful for those whose language is not read left to right, like Arabic (read right to left) and some Asian languages (read top to bottom).

1 **Practice**

- ❑ Read the directions.

- ❑ Time students for each section separately.

- ❑ At the end, ask them if their time increased, decreased, or stayed the same.

ANSWER KEY

Section 1

<u>banking</u>	banks	<u>banking</u>	bank	<u>banking</u>	<u>banking</u>
<u>challenge</u>	challenges	challenging	<u>challenge</u>	<u>challenge</u>	challenged
<u>savings</u>	<u>savings</u>	save	<u>savings</u>	saving	saver
<u>benefit</u>	benefits	beneficial	benefited	<u>benefit</u>	<u>benefit</u>
<u>employer</u>	employ	employment	employee	<u>employer</u>	employed

Time: _____

Section 2

<u>experience</u>	<u>experience</u>	experienced	expertise	<u>experience</u>	expert
<u>opening</u>	<u>opening</u>	<u>opening</u>	opened	open	opened
<u>excellent</u>	excel	excelled	<u>excellent</u>	<u>excellent</u>	<u>excellent</u>
<u>identity</u>	indent	<u>identity</u>	identify	<u>identity</u>	indent
<u>account</u>	<u>account</u>	accounting	<u>account</u>	accounts	<u>account</u>

Time: _____

Section 3

part-time	<u>part-time</u>	partly	party	<u>part-time</u>
position	possible	<u>position</u>	positive	<u>position</u>
public	<u>public</u>	publicity	<u>public</u>	publicize
appointment	appoint	appointed	appoints	<u>appointment</u>
personnel	person	personal	<u>personnel</u>	personable

Time: _____

Section 4

<u>salary</u>	<u>salary</u>	celery	salaries	salaried	sales
<u>apply</u>	applied	<u>apply</u>	<u>apply</u>	<u>apply</u>	application
<u>pleasure</u>	<u>pleasure</u>	pleasant	pleasurable	pleased	pleasant
<u>skills</u>	skilled	skill	<u>skills</u>	<u>skills</u>	skillful
<u>ability</u>	<u>ability</u>	able	capable	<u>ability</u>	capability

Time: _____

Self-Assessment Log

- ❑ Read the directions aloud and have students check vocabulary they learned in the chapter and are prepared to use.

- ❑ Have students check the strategies practiced in the chapter (or the degree to which they learned them). They have actually used all these strategies in Chapter 4.

- ❑ Put students in small groups. Ask students to find the information or an activity related to each strategy in the group.

- ❑ Tell students to find definitions in the chapter for any words they did not check.

Best Practice

Activating Prior Knowledge

Activities such as this, help students make text-to-text connections. They have previewed the vocabulary, read it in the passage, and practiced it in the activities. Making up paragraphs will help the students use the words in a slightly different context and expand their knowledge. It will also allow the teacher to see if the students have actually learned the words from the chapter. As students check each other's work, they will be reactivating their knowledge as they review an activity similar to the one they have just done.

EXPANSION ACTIVITY

- The aim of this activity is for students to practice writing words in sentences from the **Academic Word List**.

- Have the students look at the vocabulary list on page 91 and tell them each to say a word from the list in order, going through all the words to the end. Tell them to put a check (✓) beside the words they say.

- Have them take out a piece of paper and write a short paragraph containing all the words they checked, underlining the target vocabulary. Give them 10 minutes to complete the activity.

- When they have finished, collect the papers and give them to other students to read. Have the other students check them and write their names at the bottom.

- For variety, have each student write a sentence on the board from the paper that they checked. Collect the papers and check them.

Chapter

5

Lifestyles Around the World

In this chapter, students will learn about the differences between fads and trends in the first reading. They will find out which ones have been popular in North America and discuss those that have been popular in their own country. In the second reading, students will learn about fads and trends that are unconventional, like voluntary simplicity, *mehndi* and *bidis* from India, aromatherapy, and extreme sports. Later, they will also consider the questionable entertainment provided by reality TV in many countries.

Chapter Opener

- ❑ Direct students' attention to the photo on page 93 of the Student Book and ask questions: *What do you see? When/Where do you think these haircuts were popular? Which haircut do you like/ don't you like?*

- ❑ Read the quotation and ask students what it means.

- ❑ Put two words on the board: *fads* and *trends*.

- ❑ Explain that *fads* refer to things that are popular for a short time, but don't last, such as men with shaved heads. *Trends* refer to things that are popular and eventually become part of our daily life, that is, healthy living.

- ❑ Put students in pairs to list recent *fads* and *trends* in their countries.

- ❑ Call on students to share their ideas with the class.

❝ Great things are not accomplished by those who yield to trends and fads and popular opinion. ❞

—Jack Kerouac
American writer (1922–1969)

Chapter Overview

Reading Selections

Trendspotting

Fads and Trends in the 21st Century

Reading Skills and Strategies

Previewing the topic and vocabulary

Previewing the reading

Identifying the main idea

Getting meaning from context

Identifying details

Marking text when you read

Critical Thinking Skills

Organizing details using a graphic organizer

Expressing and supporting an opinion

Studying for exams: organizing information

Summarizing a paragraph

Vocabulary Building

Focusing on the Academic Word List

Analyzing suffixes and prefixes

Understanding dictionary entries: words with single and multiple meanings

Language Skills

Expressing opinions

Discussing fads and trends

Writing a paragraph

Focus on Testing

Focusing on vocabulary questions

Vocabulary

Nouns		Verbs	Adjectives	Adverbs
areas*	expert*	distinguish	creative*	enthusiastically
competitive edge	fads	enroll	irrational*	so*
culture*	lifestyle	experience	slang	suddenly
designers*	profit	invested*		
economy*	trend*	spot		
essence	trendspotting	survive*		

*These words are from the Academic Word List. For more information on this list, see www.vuw.ac.nz/lals/research/awl.

Trendspotting

Before You Read

1 Previewing the Topic

- ❏ Put students in small groups and have them look at the photos. Tell them to practice asking and answering the questions.

- ❏ Call on students to share their answers with the class. Their answers may vary.

- ❏ Write a few comments they may have about the photos on the board.

2 Previewing Vocabulary

- ❏ Read the directions to the students.

- ❏ Have them put a check (✓) next to the words they know.

- ❏ Tell them **not** to use a dictionary during this part of the lesson.

- ❏ Start the audio.

3 Previewing the Reading

- ❏ Read the questions and call on students to answer them.

- ❏ Comment on the answers, if necessary.

ANSWER KEY

Answers may vary.

1. Spotting, or finding, trends.

2. Urban Lifestyle, Fads, The Essence of a Fad, The Reason for Fads, Fads and Trends, Trendspotting, Popular Culture and the University.

3. Fads or trends in sports, entertainment, and transportation.

Read

4 Reading an Article

- ❏ On the board write *What are fads and trends, and why are they important?* and ask students to think about this question as they are reading.

- ❏ Have the students read the passage silently within a time limit (10–15 minutes), or have them follow along as you play the audio.

- ❏ Tell them to underline any words or phrases that are new or that they don't understand. Remind them **not** to use a dictionary during this part of the lesson.

- ❏ Tell students to do activity **5 Finding the Main Idea** when they finish the reading.

- ❏ Start the audio.

After You Read

5 Finding the Main Idea

- ❏ Read the directions.

- ❏ Call on different students to read the answer choices.

- ❏ Ask which one is correct.

ANSWER KEY

b. Trends, which are basically "long-lasting fads," are important for both social and business reasons.

6 **Identifying the Main Idea in Paragraphs**

- ❏ Read the directions. Tell students to look back at the reading and underline one or two sentences in each paragraph that contain the main idea.

- ❏ If students finish quickly, have them compare their answers with a partner.

- ❏ Check the answers when students finish.

7 **Checking Your Understanding**

- ❏ Read the directions and repeat the question: *What are fads and trends, and why are they important?*

- ❏ Discuss the answers that students give.

ANSWER KEY

Answers may vary.

Fads are ways of living (fashion, food, exercise) that don't last very long and are not very important. Trends are fads that last longer. They are important socially and economically. Companies that can spot a trend have a competitive edge over other companies. This means they can make money if they do it (or produce a product) before other companies.

Best Practice

Interacting with Others

Activities such as this will encourage students to use language for real-life communication and add variety to the class. Interviewing people, sharing information with the class, and transforming it into a visual message will foster fruitful interaction and meaningful language practice.

REPRODUCIBLE **EXPANSION ACTIVITY**

- ■ Photocopy and distribute **Black Line Master 13** "Fads in Your Country" on page BLM13 of this Teacher's Edition.

- ■ Tell students to interview five students and ask them about different fads in their countries.

- ■ Tell students to take notes during the interview.

- ■ Give them a few days to complete the assignment.

- ■ When they finish, have them share their findings with the class.

- ■ Compare the information to see if there are any similarities in fads among countries.

- ■ If time permits, have them look for pictures of different fads (or draw them) and make a poster for an oral presentation or for display in the classroom.

8 **Getting Meaning from Context: Vocabulary Check**

- ❏ Read the directions.

- ❏ Ask the students to repeat the words after you.

- ❏ Put them in pairs and give students a time limit (10 minutes) to find the words

- ❏ Check the answers with the class.

ANSWER KEY

Answers may vary.

1. lifestyle: *a way of living, including fashion, food, and exercise*

2. fads: *fashion that changes quickly or doesn't last long*

3. essence: *the central quality*

4. profit: *money that companies keep after their expenses are paid*

5. slang: *words or phrases that change in meaning*

6. trend: *a fad that lasts a long time and sometimes becomes an important part of our lives*

7. trendspotting: *the ability to identify a trend at an early stage*

8. competitive edge: *an advantage over other companies*

9. distinguish: *to tell the difference*

10. enroll: *to sign up to take a class*

9 **Finding Details**

❑ Read the directions.

❑ Tell students to form pairs and find the answers together.

ANSWER KEY

slang words → groovy, boss, awesome, rad, tubular

interest in health → aerobic exercise, kickboxing, organic vegetables, special diets

10 **Discussing the Reading**

❑ Read the directions.

❑ Tell students to work in pairs.

❑ Have them check the answers with another pair of students when they're finished.

ANSWER KEY

Answers may vary.

Current Fads

Clothing	Hairstyles	Food	Music	Activities
jeans / boots	sunglasses on head	white wine/sushi	Beethoven/bread	jog several miles
long skirts	shaved heads earrings	French water pasta		exercising at health clubs
natural fabrics		gourmet coffee Thai food		bicycling skateboarding
Green Peace swimsuits (old fad)		organic vegetables		"Tooth Tunes"
		special diets		aerobic exercise kickboxing
				computer games (old trend, but now part of life)

Fads and Trends in the 21st Century

Before You Read

1 Thinking Ahead

- ❑ Read the directions.
- ❑ Ask students the questions and write some of their answers on the board.

Strategy

Marking Text When You Read

- ■ Bring several highlighters to class, or ask students with them to hold them up.
- ■ Read the directions.
- ■ Ask students who have highlighters how they use them.
- ■ Suggest that all students bring at least one highlighter to class.

2 Reading: Marking Text When You Read

- ❑ Read the directions.
- ❑ Tell students who have highlighters to mark their books during this activity.
- ❑ Tell students without highlighters to underline, circle, or make notes in the margin.
- ❑ Turn on the audio.

ANSWER KEY

Answers may vary.

[A] Topic: <u>voluntary simplicity</u>
Main Idea: <u>People in the voluntary simplicity movement take various steps to make their lives both simpler and more enjoyable</u>.

[B] Topic: <u>fads from India</u>
Main Idea: <u>Wearing *mehndi* is a harmless fad, but smoking *bidis* is harmful</u>.

[C] Topic: <u>popularity of aromatherapy</u>
Main Idea: <u>Aromatherapy is a fad that uses floral and fruity scents to make people feel better</u>.

[D] Topic: <u>dangerous sports</u>
Main Idea: <u>People do variations of traditional sports that are dangerous, but they make people feel focused and alive</u>.

After You Read

3 Checking Your Answers

- ❑ Read the directions.
- ❑ Tell students to check their answers in pairs.
- ❑ Go around the room and help students with answers.

EXPANSION ACTIVITY

- ■ Photocopy and distribute **Black Line Master 14** "Extreme Sports" on page BLM14 of this Teacher's Edition.
- ■ Put students in pairs and tell them to take this paper and a pencil and go to the computer lab with a partner, or do it at home. Give them a few days to complete the assignment.
- ■ Have them look on a website for extreme sports; there a few listed on the **Black Line Master**.
- ■ Tell them to find extreme sports that they would like to try and fill in the chart.
- ■ When they finish, have them report their findings to the class.

Strategy

Studying for Exams: Organizing Information

- Read the directions.

- Demonstrate each step using this book, a notebook, and a sketch of a graphic organizer on the board.

4 **Studying for Exams: Organizing Information**

Best Practice

Organizing Information

Activities such as this will teach students to organize information from a reading passage using a graphic organizer. This allows students to better assimilate and recall information. In this case, students make note of topic, main idea, and important details.

❑ Have students work in pairs on this activity.

ANSWER KEY

Answers may vary.

	Topic	Main Idea	Important Details
A	voluntary simplicity	People in this movement are trying to make their lives simpler.	■ work less ■ move close to work ■ walk or use a bike ■ plant a veg. garden ■ buy less ■ stop buying stuff they don't need
B	fads from India	Wearing *mehndi* is harmless, but smoking *bidis* is harmful.	■ tattoos are permanent ■ parents are horrified ■ young people like them ■ *mehndi* is temporary ■ young people smoke *bidis* ■ they have candy flavors ■ parent worry about this
C	popularity of aromatherapy	Aromatherapy uses scents to make people feel better.	■ perfume attracts people ■ we remember smells ■ floral scents are pleasant ■ people feel better ■ it's a good business
D	dangerous sports	People do dangerous sports that make them feel focused and alive.	■ sports are made dangerous ■ snowboarding, mountain biking ■ thrill seekers like them ■ "extreme sports" created ■ sky-surfing, waterfall-running ■ feel focused and alive

5 Discussing the Reading

- ❏ Read the directions.
- ❏ Divide students into small groups to discuss the answers.
- ❏ Have them share their answers with the class.

Responding in Writing

6 Summarizing

- ❏ Read the directions.
- ❏ Ask two students to read Summary 1 and Summary 2.
- ❏ Have them compare the summaries with Paragraph A on page 101.
- ❏ Discuss the differences.

7 Writing Your Own Summary

- ❏ Tell students to choose one of the paragraphs listed to summarize.
- ❏ Remind them not to look at the original paragraph as they are writing. Tell those who have chosen Paragraphs B and C to look at the graphic organizer on page 104 to help them with their summary.
- ❏ Give students 15–20 minutes for this activity.
- ❏ Have students who worked on the same paragraph compare their summaries when finished.
- ❏ Collect summaries and check.

8 Responding in Writing

Best Practice

Activating Prior Knowledge

An activity such as writing a summary in class enables students to be more successful when they work at home. This activity uses prior practice as a scaffold, enabling students be more successful when they write a summary by themselves.

- ❏ Assign the paragraph in this section for homework, allowing each student to choose a topic.
- ❏ Tell students to write the main idea on the line in their books.
- ❏ Before you collect the homework, tell students to exchange papers and read their partner's paragraph.
- ❏ Ask them to write the main idea under the paragraph.
- ❏ When students get their papers back, have them compare their main idea with the one their partners wrote under their paragraph.
- ❏ Collect the papers and correct.

Talk It Over

9 **Reality TV: What Do You Think?**

Best Practice

Cultivating Critical Thinking

Activities such as this prepare students for discussing present-day issues. By discussing topics like reality TV shows from different countries, students engage in critical thinking and are able to formulate their own opinions after considering the content, the viewers, and the reasons for the current popularity of these shows.

❏ Read the directions.

❏ Put students into small groups.

❏ Tell them to discuss the questions.

❏ Have them share their answers with the class.

❏ This theme is continued in the **Expansion Activity** on page 71 of the Teacher's Edition.

1 **Focusing on Words from the Academic Word List**

❑ Read the directions.

❑ Say the words and have students repeat them after you.

❑ Ask them what part of speech the words are and tell them to write *n.*, *v.*, *adj.*, or *adv.* after the words.

❑ Tell them to cross off the words from the list as they fill in the blanks.

❑ Check the answers.

areas – n	culture – n
economy – n	irrational – adj
creative – adj	designers – n
expert – n/adj	so – adv

ANSWER KEY

1. so 2. designers 3. areas 4. expert 5. culture
6. irrational 7. creative 8. economy

ANALYZING SUFFIXES

■ Write the suffixes from the box on the board.

Nouns	Verbs	Adjective	Adverb
____-ess	____-ate	____-less	____-ly
____-ship	____-ize		
____-ism	____-en		

■ Read the information.

■ Ask students to go to the board and write some words in the columns containing these suffixes, or elicit them from the students.

2 **Analyzing Suffixes**

❑ Read the directions.

❑ Remind the students **not** to use a dictionary during this activity.

❑ Check the answers when students have finished.

ANSWER KEY

1. n 2. adv 3. n 4. v 5. n 6. v 7. n 8. adj 9. adv
10. adj 11. v 12. n 13. v 14. adj 15. v 16. adv
17. n 18. v 19. n 20. n 21. n 22. n/v 23. n
24. adj

ANALYZING PREFIXES

■ Write the example from the box on the board.

We've <u>discovered</u> many <u>un</u>usual hotels in our travels.

■ Write the prefixes from the box in columns across the board.

un-

in-

im-

ir-

dis-

■ Read the information.

■ Ask students to go to the board and write some words in the columns containing these prefixes, or elicit them from the students.

3 **Analyzing Prefixes**

❑ Read the directions.

❑ Check answers when finished.

ANSWER KEY

1. un 2. im 3. in 4. un 5. un 6. ir 7. un 8. in
9. un 10. dis 11. im 12. un

MORE PREFIXES

- Write the prefixes on the board without the meanings, as in the previous activity.

- Explain that these prefixes come from Latin and that many Latinate languages (French, Italian, Portuguese, and Spanish) have similar prefixes.

- Ask students to go to the board and write words in the columns containing these prefixes, or elicit them from students.

con-/com- = with, together   *pre-* = first, before

counter- = opposite   *re-* = again, back

ex-/e- = out of, from   *sur-* = over, above

inter- = between, among   *trans-* = across

mis- = wrong

Best Practice

Scaffolding Instruction

This activity uses the students' prior knowledge as a scaffold. It helps them place what they already know about prefixes in their own language into the understanding and use of prefixes in English.

4 Matching Words

- Read the directions.
- Have the students do the activity without using a dictionary.
- Check the answers.

ANSWER KEY

1. g 2. i 3. c 4. a 5. j 6. b 7. e 8. d 9. h 10. f

5 Understanding Dictionary Entries: Single Meanings

- Read the directions.

- Ask two students to read the two dictionary entries, or tell students to read them silently.

- Ask other students to answer the questions.

ANSWER KEY

1. verb 2. to make (oneself or another person) officially a member of a group, school, and so on 3. enrollment 4. noun 5. a short-lived interest or practice

6 Understanding Dictionary Entries: Multiple Meanings

- Read the directions.

- Ask several students to read the parts of the dictionary entry, or tell students to read it silently.

- Ask other students to answer the questions.

ANSWER KEY

1. noun/*the style of the 1930s* 2. a. noun b. noun c. verb 3. a. in a particular way b. a general way of doing something c. to cut one's hair in a particular way d. a type or sort, esp. of goods.

7 Dictionary Practice

Best Practice

Making Use of Academic Content

Activities such as this will help expand students' use of the dictionary (paperback, electronic, or online) from a mere translator into a more useful tool that can help them learn about parts of speech, different meanings of words, and examples.

❑ Read the directions.

❑ Tell students to work as quickly as possible.

❑ If students finish quickly, have them check their answers with a partner.

ANSWER KEY

1. adj. – without anything added or without decoration
2. n. – large area of flat land
3. adj. – quick to see and act; watchful
4. v. – to warn
5. n. – a strong upright pole or bar made of wood, metal, and so on, usually fixed into the ground
6. v. – to make public or show by fixing to a wall, board, post, or other material

8 Searching the Internet

❑ Read the directions.

❑ Put students in pairs and tell them to choose a country where they can look for a reality TV show. List the countries on the board so they are not duplicated.

❑ Send students to the computer lab or tell them to do the assignment for homework.

REPRODUCIBLE EXPANSION ACTIVITY

■ Photocopy and distribute **Black Line Master 15** "Reality TV Shows" on page BLM15 of this Teacher's Edition.

■ Put students into pairs and have them look on the Internet for reality TV shows in the country they have chosen.

■ Tell them to choose a show, find out what it's about, and write a summary like those in the **Culture Note**, page 106.

■ If the show is still being shown, have them explain who the participants are. If it has ended, have them explain how it ended.

■ Tell them to include their opinion of the show on the sheet.

■ Give them a few days to complete the assignment and have them share their findings with the class.

VOCABULARY QUESTIONS

- Read the directions to students.

- Tell the students that they will do an activity that will help prepare them for the iBT.

1 Practice

❑ Read the directions.

❑ Write *"Trendspotting," pages 95–98*, and *Practice, page 113*, on the board.

❑ Put the current time and the time in ten minutes on the board, for example, 10:30–10:40.

❑ Tell the students to begin the **Practice**, working as quickly as possible.

ANSWER KEY

1. b 2. d 3. a 4. c 5. a 6. b 7. d 8. d

Self-Assessment Log

❑ Read the directions aloud and have students check vocabulary they learned in the chapter and are prepared to use.

❑ Have students check the strategies practiced in the chapter (or the degree to which they learned them). They have actually used all these strategies in Chapter 5.

❑ Put students in small groups. Ask students to find the information or an activity related to each strategy in the group.

❑ Tell students to find definitions in the chapter for any words they did not check.

Best Practice

Interacting with Others

Activities such as this will energize the students and add excitement to the class. Since most interaction in this chapter has been in pairs or small groups, students will enjoy a change of pace with competitive interaction.

EXPANSION ACTIVITY

- Write all the words from the **Target Vocabulary** list on separate pieces of paper.

- Divide the students into 4 groups, and give each group 4 pieces of paper with words from the list. Tell them not to let the other groups know which words they have.

- Tell them to look up their words in a dictionary and write the meanings on the back of each piece of paper.

- Have each group go to the board and write the definition of one of the words on the board.

- Tell the other groups to guess the word without looking at the list.

- The group that guesses the word first gets a point and puts one of their definitions on the board.

- Repeat this process until none of the groups have any more words.

- Tally the score at the end. The team with the highest score wins.

- If it's not possible for the students to go to the board, tell them to stand up and say the definition and have the groups guess.

6
Global Connections

In this chapter, students will learn about global trade in the first reading and the advantages and disadvantages it brings to developed and developing countries. They will also read about the influence of geography and protectionist policies on trade. Students will learn about global travel in the second reading and the variety of experiences available to travelers today. Trains, boats, and planes take travelers on mystery tours, ecotours, scientific adventures, and—for those with enough money—even into space!

Chapter Opener

- ❏ Direct students' attention to the photo on page 117 of the Student Book and ask questions: *What do you see? Where do you think this is? Could this be a scene from your country?*

- ❏ Read the quotation and ask students what it means.

- ❏ Put these words on the board: *globalization, protectionism, infrastructure*.

- ❏ Divide students into small groups and ask them to guess what these words mean. Have them generate a list of words that they associate with these concepts.

- ❏ Elicit words from the students and write them on the board.

❝ It has been said that arguing against globalization is like arguing against the laws of gravity. ❞

—Kofi Annan
Ghanaian diplomat; seventh Secretary
General of the United Nations (1938–)

Chapter Overview

Reading Selections

Global Trade

Global Travel. . . and Beyond

Reading Skills and Strategies

Previewing the topic and vocabulary

Identifying the main ideas

Skimming for main ideas

Critical Thinking Skills

Understanding the literal and figurative meanings
of words

Organizing information using an outline

Summarizing in writing

Identifying inferences

Vocabulary Building

Focusing on the Academic Word List

Understanding idioms

Focusing on expressions and idioms

Using participles as adjectives

Language Skills

Stating and explaining opinions

Writing a paragraph

Focus on Testing

Identifying inferences

Vocabulary

Nouns	Verbs	Adjectives	Idioms and Expressions
benefits*	created*	economic*	get around
fuel	reduce	global*	hands on
gap	require*	landlocked	hold (someone) back
goods			in the market for
harbor			on board
infrastructure*			on your own
nutrients			private eye
obstacle			pulled into
policies (policy)*			rough it
priority*			runs
protectionist policies			take (one's) time
subsidy*			track down
technology*			whodunit
tide			

*These words are from the Academic Word List. For more information on this list,
see www.vuw.ac.nz/lals/research/awl.

Global Trade

Before You Read

1 Previewing the Topic

- ❏ Put students in small groups and have them discuss the questions.
- ❏ Call on students to share their answers with the class. Their answers may vary.
- ❏ Write a few comments they may have about the discussion on the board.

2 Previewing Vocabulary

- ❏ Read the directions to the students.
- ❏ Have them put a check (✓) next to the words they know.
- ❏ Tell them **not** to use a dictionary during this part of the lesson.
- ❏ Start the audio.

3 Previewing

- ❏ Read the questions and have students work in pairs to answer them.
- ❏ Give them a time limit of 5 minutes to answer the questions.
- ❏ Call on students to answer the questions so you can check their answers.
- ❏ Comment on the answers, if necessary.

ANSWER KEY

Answers may vary.

1. Global trade
2. Open Trade, "Leaking Boats," The Influence of Geography, Protectionist Policies, A Way Out.
3. Infotech workers in India.

Read

4 Reading the Article

- ❏ Read the directions.
- ❏ Write *"What seems to be the main key to a country's economic success?"* on the board and ask students to think about this question as they are reading.
- ❏ Have students read the passage silently within a time limit (10–15 minutes) or have them follow along silently as you play the audio.
- ❏ Tell them to underline any words or phrases that are new or that they don't understand. Remind them **not** to use a dictionary during this part of the lesson.
- ❏ Tell the students to look at the activity following the reading if they finish quickly.
- ❏ Turn on the audio.

After You Read

5 Finding the Main Ideas

- ❏ Read the directions.
- ❏ Call on different students to read the answer choices.
- ❏ Ask if the answers are true or false.

ANSWER KEY

1. T 2. F 3. T 4. F 5. T

Strategy

Understanding the Literal and Figurative Meanings of Words

- ■ Write *literal = letters* and *figurative = form or figure*.
- ■ Write the sentence from the **Strategy Box** on the board:

  *The woman with the sad **face** is worried about how to **face** the future.*

- Draw a simple figure of a woman with a sad face in profile facing right.

- On her left write *past*, and on her right, write *future*.

- Explain that the literal meaning of the noun, *face*, is a person's face, and the figurative meaning of the verb, *to face*, is to look toward or confront.

- Tell students that many words have both literal and figurative meanings.

6 **Understanding the Literal and Figurative Meanings of Words**

❑ Read the directions. Tell students to look back at the reading to find the answers. Give them a time limit (10 min.).

❑ Check the answers when students finish.

ANSWER KEY

1. d 2. a 3. c 4. d 5. b 6. d 7. d 8. c

7 **Checking Vocabulary**

❑ Read the directions.

❑ Check the answers when the students finish.

ANSWER KEY

1. benefits 2. in turn 3. goods 4. fuel
5. reduce 6. tide 7. harbor 8. gap 9. landlocked
10. nutrients 11. obstacle 12. it goes without
saying 13. protectionist policies 14. subsidy
15. infrastructure

8 **Checking Your Understanding**

❑ Read the directions.

❑ Discuss the answers that students give and write some of them on the board.

Understanding Outlines

- Write the first section of the outline on the board:

Global Trade

I. Introduction: Benefits of Open Trade
  A. For developed countries
    1. More competition
    2. Lower prices
    3. More consumer choice
  B. For developing countries—access to essential goods
  C. For both
    1. Reduce poverty
    2. Improve living conditions

- Read the directions.

- Ask a student to read paragraph [A] on page 119. Tell students to listen and look at the outline on the board.

- Point out the phrases on the board as the student reads them.

- Ask these questions and tell the students to answer them using the phrases on the board:

  What are the benefits of open trade for developed countries?

  What are the benefits of open trade for developing countries?

  What are the benefits of open trade for both countries?

- Have the students silently read the remainder of the outline.

9 **Understanding Outlines**

Organizing Information

Activities such as this will teach students to organize information using an outline. This allows students to identify main ideas and supporting details from sections of text and put it into a format that facilitates review at a later date.

❏ Read the directions.

❏ Tell students to do the activity using the outline on pages 124–125.

ANSWER KEY

1. global trade 2. more competition, lower prices, more consumer choice 3. "leaking boats," wider gap between rich and poor 4. agricultural subsidies, "hidden" protectionist policies
5. create an economic climate in which people can move from agriculture to manufacturing and infotech; pay attention to infrastructure and education, and persuade developed countries to drop protectionist policies

Best Practice

Cultivating Critical Thinking

Activities such as this allow students to engage in critical thinking as they consider the current state of affairs in countries around the world. By doing research on the Internet and identifying a country's resources, industries, and income, they will be better able to formulate ideas about its assets and liabilities in order to assess its capacity for economic success.

EXPANSION ACTIVITY

■ Photocopy and distribute **Black Line Master 16** "Analyzing a Country" on page BLM16 of this Teacher's Edition.

■ Tell students to choose a country, either their own or another one.

■ Keep a list of the countries to make sure that each one is different.

■ In pairs, have students look on the Internet at a website such as these:

http://www.nationsonline.org
http://www.infoplease.com/countries.html
http://www.cia.gov/cia/publications/factbook

■ Give them a few days to complete the assignment.

■ When they finish, have them share their findings with the class.

■ If time permits, have them look for pictures (or draw them) and make a poster for an oral presentation or for display in the classroom.

■ Write these questions on the board before the presentations, telling them to analyze the success of the country, comparing their country to the ones presented by the other students.

In which areas is this country economically successful?
Which factors contribute to this success?
In which areas is it not so successful?
What predictions can you make about the country's future?

■ Invite students to ask questions or make comments on the presentations.

10 Finding the Main Idea

❏ Read the question.

❏ Call on different students to read the answer choices.

❏ Elicit the answer **(E)**.

11 Discussing the Reading

❏ Read the directions.

❏ Divide the students into pairs or small groups.

❏ Go around the room and listen to the discussion.

❏ Ask students to share their ideas with the class.

Global Travel . . . and Beyond

Before You Read

1 Thinking Ahead

> **Best Practice**
>
> **Scaffolding Instruction**
> Activities such as this will allow students to better understand a reading by scaffolding instruction. Eliciting information that students already know will enable them to understand new information and integrate it with prior knowledge.

❑ Read the directions.

❑ Write these words on the board in a T-chart (see page 10 in the Student Book for information about T-charts).

Types of Travel	Places to Go	Obstacles

❑ Ask students the questions and write some of their answers in the three columns.

❑ After the reading, call students' attention to the chart to see if their ideas were found in the reading.

❑ Put a check (✓) beside those that were.

Read

2 Identifying the Main Ideas

❑ Read the directions.

❑ Give students a time limit (10–15 minutes) or turn on the audio.

❑ Check the answers.

ANSWER KEY

[A] b [B] d [C] a [D] a [E] b [F] e

After You Read

UNDERSTANDING IDIOMS

■ Write these sentences on the board and underline the idioms:

> *Our trip was <u>out of this world</u>. We spent a fabulous week on the island of Bali. We stayed <u>on board</u> a boat and <u>got around</u> by sailing to different towns. We <u>roughed it</u> by catching fish and eating them.*

■ Ask a student to read the first paragraph in the box.

■ Read the sentences on the board, point out the idioms, and explain them.

■ Ask another student to read the second paragraph.

3 Understanding Idioms

❑ Read the directions.

❑ Tell students to do the activity in pairs.

❑ Go around the room and help students with answers, if necessary.

ANSWER KEY

Answers may vary.

1. stop the progress or movement of (A): *hold (someone) back*
2. alone; not with a group (A): *on (one's) own*
3. looking for; hoping to find (A): *in the market for*
4. travels; goes (B): *runs*
5. on a train (B): *on board*
6. detective (B): *private eye*
7. look for and find (B): *track down*
8. mystery (B): *whodunit*
9. arrived in (B): *pulled into*
10. travel in a simple and not comfortable way (C): *rough it*

11. go from place to place (C): _get around_

12. with direct and active participation [C]: _hands-on experience_

13. travel slowly [C]: _take (one's) time_

Responding in Writing

4 Summarizing

❑ Read the directions.

❑ Give students a minute to decide which part they will write about.

❑ Ask students who are going to summarize a paragraph from Part 1 to sit on one side of the room. Ask students who are going to summarize a paragraph from Part 2 to sit on the other side of the room.

❑ Write these two pieces of advice on the board: _"A summary is shorter than the original."_ and _"Don't look at the original paragraph as you write."_

❑ Put students in pairs. They can first write the summary alone, and then compare their summary with that of their partner.

❑ When they have compared their summaries, collect the summaries and check them.

5 Writing Your Own Ideas

Best Practice

Interacting with Others

Activities such as this will encourage students to use language for real-life communication and add variety to the class. Writing a letter and getting an answer from a classmate will foster meaningful interaction and interesting language practice.

❑ Read the directions.

❑ Have students choose one of the topics listed and write the letter for homework.

❑ Write this format on the board and tell students to copy it:

> 2/18/08
>
> Dear _____ ,
>
> I'm planning to go on a trip to . . . _(Describe this type of travel, but do not copy from the reading.)_
>
> Would you like to go with me? _(Tell your friend why he/she would enjoy the trip.)_
>
> Your friend,
> Kazuyo

❑ The next day, collect the letters.

❑ Pass them around to different students in the class. Make sure no one gets his or her own letter.

❑ Tell the students to read them and write the main idea of each paragraph at the bottom.

❑ Then have the students write a response to the letter on the back of the paper, telling why they _would_ or _would not_ like to go on the trip.

❑ When students finish, they can give the letters back to the person who wrote them.

❑ After they have read the letters, collect and check them.

6 Discussing the Reading

❑ Read the directions.

❑ Divide students into small groups to discuss the answers.

❑ Have them share their answers with the class.

7 Searching the Internet

Best Practice

Activating Prior Knowledge

Activities such as looking for a new vacation adventure with a partner or small group enables students to use their imagination and planning skills. This activity uses prior knowledge of previous vacations, enabling students to choose a similar or different kind of trip and enjoy planning their activities.

❑ Read the directions.

❑ Have students look at the travel choices in Activity 5.

❑ Ask them to choose one and find a partner who chose the same one.

❑ Tell them to do the **Expansion Activity** together.

 EXPANSION ACTIVITY

■ Photocopy and distribute **Black Line Master 17** "A Different Kind of Vacation" on page BLM17 of this Teacher's Edition.

■ Put students who chose the same type of travel into pairs or small groups.

■ Have them go to the computer lab or do the activity at home.

■ Give them a few days to finish the assignment.

■ Tell the students they can either make a poster or a PowerPoint presentation of their trip.

■ Have them give the presentation to the class.

1 Focusing on Words from the Academic Word List

❑ Read the directions.

❑ Say the words and have students repeat them after you.

❑ Ask them what part of speech they are and tell them to write n, v, adj, or adv after the words.

❑ Tell them to cross off the words from the list as they fill in the blanks.

❑ Check the answers.

areas – n	global – adj	policy – n
created – v	infrastructure – n	priority – n
economic – adj	policies – n	require – v
technology – n		

ANSWER KEY

1. global 2. economic 3. policy 4. created
5. areas 6. infrastructure 7. technology
8. require 9. priority 10. policies

2 Expressions and Idioms

❑ Read the directions.

❑ Say the expressions and have the students repeat them after you.

❑ Remind the students **not** to use a dictionary during this activity.

❑ Check the answers when students have finished.

ANSWER KEY

1. hold back 2. get around 3. private eye
4. track down 5. in the market for 6. rough it
7. goes without saying 8. out of this world

USING PARTICIPLES AS ADJECTIVES

■ Write the adjectives and the verbs from the box on the board:

Present Participle	**Past Participle**
-ing = cause of emotion	-ed = effect or result
That book is *interesting*.	I'm *interested* in that book.
We watched a *boring* movie.	We were so *bored* that we fell asleep.
The race was *tiring*.	The runners were *tired* after it.

■ Read the information.

■ Call on two students to read the **Examples**.

3 Using Participles as Adjectives

❑ Read the directions.

❑ Say the expressions and have the students give you the present and past participle. For example, when you say *addict*, students say *addicting—addicted*; *challenging/challenged*; *exciting/excited*; *frightening/frightened*; *horrifying/horrified*; *interesting/interested*; *relaxing/relaxed*; *terrifying/terrified*; *thrilling/ thrilled*; *tiring/tired*

❑ Have students work on the activity in pairs.

❑ Check answers when finished.

ANSWER KEY

Answers may vary.

1. interested; challenging

2. tiring; tired; relaxing; relaxed

3. exciting/thrilling; excited; terrified; terrifying/ frightening

4. thrilling; addicted; thrilled; horrified/frightened

UNDERSTANDING INFERENCES

- Read the paragraph to students.

- Tell the students that they will do two activities that will help prepare them for the iBT.

1 Practice

- ❏ Read the directions, emphasizing that each one has several answers.

- ❏ Write *"Global Trade,"* pages 119–121, on the board.

- ❏ Put the current time and the time in ten minutes on the board, for example, 10:30–10:40.

- ❏ Tell the students to begin the activity, working as quickly as possible.

ANSWER KEY

1. a, c, d 2. a, b, e 3. b, c, d 4. a, c, e

2 Critical Thinking: Identifying Inferences

Best Practice

Making Use of Academic Content

Activities such as this will help expand students' understanding of inference in academic texts. With practice, they will learn to recognize what can be inferred from factual information.

- ❏ Read the directions.

- ❏ Point out the answer in the first item.

- ❏ Tell the students to use highlighters to find the phrases in the reading, if possible.

- ❏ Then have the students check the statements where they have found the phrases from which they inferred the information and write them on the lines.

- ❏ Check the answers when students have finished.

ANSWER KEY

Answers may vary.

Paragraph A

1. _✓_ You don't have to be rich to travel.
   not all travel is expensive, so lack of money doesn't have to hold people back

2. _✓_ It costs a lot of money to take a cruise.
   they think of expensive cruise ships

3. _✓_ There is greater variety today in types of travel than there used to be.
   there is an enormous variety of possibilities for people of all interests

4. _____ It's better to travel on your own than in a group.

Paragraph B

1. _✓_ Today, train travel is more than just a way to get from place to place.
   It can also offer education or adventure

2. _____ The Trans-Siberian Special is a lot of fun.

3. _____ The Murder Mystery Trains are expensive.

4. _✓_ The Murder Mystery Trains are fun.
   For people who are looking for fun and adventure, there are the Murder Mystery Trains of Western Australia.

Paragraph C

1. _✓_ Ecotourism is popular with some people.
   approximately 20 percent of all international travel is now nature travel

2. _✓_ Ecotours are often not very comfortable.
   they don't expect hot showers, clean sheets, gourmet food, or air-conditioned houses

3. _✓_ Serious ecotourists care about animals.
   Serious ecotourists are interested in preserving the environment and learning about wildlife.

4. _✓_ Ecotourists don't enjoy comfortable hotels.
   Many travelers choose to rough it.

Paragraph D

1. __✓__ Earthwatch doesn't have any projects in the arts.
you learn a specific science in a hands-on experience

2. __✓__ There is a variety of subjects that people can study in different countries.
projects change from year to year, but among typical possibilities are digging up dinosaur bones, building solar ovens, or studying medicinal plants

3. _____ Rich people prefer to take courses, and people without money prefer to volunteer.

4. __✓__ An Earthwatch project is a valuable experience for a person who is trying to decide what subject to select as a major in college.
they can try out a potential career

Paragraph E

1. __✓__ Cruise ships are expensive.
People who don't have money for a cruise ship

2. _____ A freighter is a kind of ship.
People who enjoy ocean travel . . . might try a freighter

3. _____ Freighters are as exciting as cruise ships.

4. __✓__ Travel by freighter is probably not good for people who are in a hurry
For people who want to take their time, it's a relaxing way to travel

Paragraph F

1. __✓__ The expression _out of this world_ has both a literal and a figurative meaning.
By this idiom, they mean their trip was amazing or wonderful

2. _____ The feeling of weightlessness is always enjoyable for all people.

3. __✓__ Most people probably cannot afford a week on the International Space Station.
at a price of $20,000,000 each

4. _____ Space hotels will be comfortable.

Self-Assessment Log

❏ Read the directions aloud and have students check vocabulary they learned in the chapter and are prepared to use.

❏ Have students check the strategies practiced in the chapter (or the degree to which they learned them). They have actually used all these strategies in Chapter 6.

❏ Put students in small groups. Ask students to find the information or an activity related to each strategy in the group.

❏ Tell students to find definitions in the chapter for any words they did not check.

EXPANSION ACTIVITY

■ Write the expressions from the left column of **PART 2–3 Understanding Idioms**, page 131, on the board.

■ Write the words from right column on separate pieces of paper and distribute them to students or pairs of students, depending on the number in class. Add other words from the list, if necessary.

■ Divide students into 2 teams, making sure they keep their books closed.

■ Tell them to look at the expressions on the board and allow one student/pair to go to the board to write their idiom.

■ If it's not possible for the students to go to the board, read the sentences aloud one by one and have students stand up and say their idiom if it fits in the sentence.

■ If it is correct, give the team a point, and have a member/pair of the other team go to the board.

■ Repeat this process until neither team has any more words.

■ Tally the score at the end. The team with the highest score wins.

■ Photocopy and distribute **Black Line Master 18** "Matching Idioms" on page BLM18 of this Teacher's Edition.

■ Tell students to copy down the answers on the **Black Line Master** and study for the chapter test.

7

Language and Communication

In this chapter, students will read about different aspects of language and communication, such as how animals communicate, how human communication differs according to gender, and finally, how English is changing as it spreads around the world. In the first reading, they will learn about the communication of insects through smell and sight, the vocalizations of prairie dogs and dolphins, the ability of chimpanzees to communicate through body language and manipulation of symbols, like humans. They will explore the differences between male and female styles of communication, as studied by the noted linguist, Deborah Tannen, and discuss these differences with their classmates. At the end of the chapter, they will learn of the dismay of linguists at the morphing of the Queen's English into different hybrids around the world. These topics will encourage students to think about modes of communication among animals and humans as well as the language they are in the process of acquiring.

Chapter Opener

❑ Direct students' attention to the photo on page 141 of the Student Book and ask questions: *What do you see? What are they doing? How do people communicate with each other?*

❑ Read the quotation by Whorf and ask students what it means.

❑ Put this sentence on the board: *People who speak English think differently from people who speak* _____ . Tell students to put their native language in the blank.

❑ Put students from different language groups in pairs (if possible) to discuss the sentence.

❑ Call on students to share their ideas with the class.

❝ Language shapes the way we think and determines what we think about. ❞

—Benjamin Lee Whorf
American linguist, (1897–1941)

Chapter Overview

Reading Selections
If We Could Talk with Animals . . .
"Parentese"

Reading Skills and Strategies
Previewing the topic and vocabulary
Previewing the reading
Identifying the main ideas
Identifying details
Getting meaning from context
Understanding italics and quotation marks
Skimming for main ideas

Critical Thinking Skills
Categorizing
Interpreting a photograph
Identifying details and analyzing material using graphic organizers

Identifying inferences
Distinguishing facts from assumptions
Summarizing a paragraph

Vocabulary Building
Understanding homophones
Focusing on the Academic Word List
Working with prefixes and suffixes
Understanding words in phrases
Learning new vocabulary: making a vocabulary log

Language Skills
Discussing the nature/nurture question
Writing a paragraph

Focus on Testing
Focusing on comprehension questions about details

Vocabulary

Nouns		Verbs	Adjectives	Adverbs	Idioms and Expressions
brain	mammals	acquire*	identical*	apparently*	head (of something)
capacity*	nature	claims	verbal	percent*	head back
chatter	nurture	coin		upright	picked up
communication*	organs	feeds			shedding light on
context*	pod	focusing*			
creatures	prey	realize			
degree	primates	reassure			
emotions	research*	respond*			
evidence*	situation	vocalize			
gender*	species	wagging			
gestures	structures*				
glue	subjects				
grin	swagger				
journal*					

*These words are from the Academic Word List. For more information on this list, see www.vuw.ac.nz/lals/research/awl.

If We Could Talk with Animals . . .

Before You Read

1 Previewing the Topic

- ❏ Have students look at the photos.

- ❏ Have them read the questions and write brief answers.

- ❏ Put students in pairs to practice asking and answering questions.

- ❏ Call on students to share their answers with the class.

EXPANSION ACTIVITY

REPRODUCIBLE

- ■ The aim of this activity is for students to find out more about each other and begin thinking about the theme of this chapter.

- ■ Photocopy and distribute **Black Line Master 19** "Find Someone Who…" on page BLM19 of this Teacher's Edition.

- ■ Model the activity. Call on a student and ask: *Do you have a dog?* Continue asking until someone answers *yes*. Ask: *How does it communicate with you?* Listen to the answer. Point out that when students find someone who answers *yes*, they can write that person's name on the line.

- ■ Have students walk around the room and ask questions until they write someone's name next to each item. Point out that they can use a classmates' name only once.

- ■ When students complete the worksheet, ask each one to tell the class something he or she learned (*Ming has a bird, and it sings to her.*).

---

2 Previewing Vocabulary

- ❏ Read the directions to the students.

- ❏ Have them put a check (✓) next to the words they know.

- ❏ Remind them **not** to use a dictionary during this part of the lesson.

- ❏ Tell them to put the stress on words of more than one syllable as they listen to the audio.

- ❏ Write these words on the board as examples: *chat'ter, gen'der, swag'ger*.

- ❏ Start the audio.

- ❏ Have the students write the words on the board, marking the stress.

ANSWER KEY

Nouns	Verbs
brain	acquire'
chat'ter	claims
crea'tures	coin
degree'	ech'oes
ech'o	feeds
gen'der	reassure'
ges'tures	vo'calize
grin	wag'ging
lex'igrams	**Adverb**
mam'mals	up'right
or'gans	
pod	**Idioms and Expressions**
prey	head (of something)
prim'ates	head back'
spe'cies	picked up'
sub'jects	shedding light' on
swag'ger	

---

3 Previewing the Reading

- ❏ Put students in pairs to practice asking and answering the questions.

- ❏ Call on students to share their answers with the class. Their answers may vary.

- ❏ Write on the board a few of the questions they may have about the reading.

Read

4 Reading the Article

- ❑ On the board write *"How do animals communicate? Do animals have the capacity to learn language?"* and ask students to think about this question and the other questions you have written on the board as they are reading.

- ❑ Have the students read the passage silently within a time limit (10–15 minutes), or have them follow along as you play the audio.

- ❑ Tell them to underline any words or phrases that are new or that they don't understand. Remind them **not** to use a dictionary during this part of the lesson.

- ❑ Tell students to think about the questions on the board if they finish the reading quickly.

- ❑ Start the audio.

- ❑ When the time limit is reached or the audio is finished, point to the questions on the board and ask students if they found the answers.

Content Note

- ■ Dr. Doolittle, a character invented by the British writer Hugh Lofting (1886–1947), was a veterinarian who could communicate with animals, even imaginary ones. Eddie Murphy made two comedy films based on this character in 1998 and 2001.

- ■ Dr. Jane Goodall is a primatologist who has studied the behavior of chimpanzees in Tanzania, Africa, since 1960. She was the first to document that chimps used tools, hunted for meat, and had diverse personalities. She has taught and lectured about chimps all over the world.

- ■ Dr. Con Slobodchikoff is a professor of biology at the University of Northern Arizona. He has studied colonies of prairie dogs and interpreted the alarm calls they use to protect the colony from predators.

- ■ Dr. Louis Herman founded the Dolphin Institute at the Marine Mammal Laboratory of the University of Hawaii over 30 years ago. He studied these intelligent animals to learn more about their cognitive, behavioral, and sensory capabilities.

- ■ Dr. Noam Chomsky has been a professor of linguistics at the Massachusetts Institute of Technology (MIT) for many decades. His seminal work, *Transformational Analysis*, changed the way linguists thought about grammar and speech.

After You Read

5 Getting the Main Ideas

- ❑ Read the directions and call on one student to read the first statement. Ask the class for the answer.

- ❑ Have the students continue with the rest of the statements individually. Students can check their answers with a partner if they finish quickly.

- ❑ Finish checking the answers as a class.

ANSWER KEY

1. T 2. F 3. F 4. T 5. F 6. T 7. F

6 Checking Your Understanding

Best Practice

Interacting with Others

These types of collaborative activities help students get a better understanding of the ideas in the reading passage through interacting with other students. They can clarify answers and reinforce knowledge with the assistance of their group members.

❑ Divide students into small groups for this activity. Read the directions.

❑ Tell students to work together by identifying the paragraphs in which the answers can be found and underlining the sentences.

❑ Circulate and help students if necessary.

ANSWER KEY

1. Animals communicate by using smell, body language, and vocalizations. [Subtitles of paragraphs B, C, and D]

2. Dolphins have been taught a language of hand symbols. [F] Chimps have been taught to understand and use American Sign Language (ASL) and symbols on a keyboard (lexigrams). [G]

3. Dogs wag their tails when they're happy and put their chest on the floor and rear end in the air when they want to play. Chimps swagger and wave their arms or throw branches when they're angry; they lower themselves to the ground and hold out their hands or show their rear ends when they're nervous in the presence of a more powerful chimp; a more powerful chimp touches, hugs, or kisses a nervous chimp to reassure her; when chimps are nervous or fearful, they "smile" by showing their teeth in a grin similar to one humans make. [C]

4. Biological evidence shows that an area of the brain in chimps, the *planum temporale*, is essentially identical to that of humans. [I]

7 Getting Meaning from Context

❑ On the board, put the phrase *Clues to Meaning*. Under it, write the following punctuations marks (words and symbols) and expressions:

> commas , _____ ,
> parentheses (_____)
> dashes – _____ –
>
> *in other words*
> *that is/i.e. (id est in Latin)*

❑ Tell students to look for these punctuation marks and expressions when they see words or phrases they don't understand. These clues to meaning will help them understand new words and phrases.

❑ Read the directions and the first example.

ANSWER KEY

1. shedding light on 2. head back 3. gestures
4. wagging 5. upright 6. swagger 7. grin
8. reassure 9. vocalize 10. prey 11. pod
12. species 13. chatter 14. claims 15. gender
16. mammals 17. acquire 18. brain

8 Categorizing

❑ Read the directions.

❑ Give students a time limit (5 minutes). Check answers when they have finished.

ANSWER KEY

1. creatures 2. primates

UNDERSTANDING HOMOPHONES

■ On the board, write the word *homophone* and the Greek roots: *homo = same* and *phone = sound*. Explain that it is a word that sounds the same, but with two or more different meanings. Sometimes homophones have the same spelling.

■ Write these examples on the board and explain to students:

> The *chair* of the biology department sat in the most comfortable *chair*.

> The chimp found a *quarter* on the floor; then he ate a *quarter* of an apple.

■ Call on students to read the examples in the book.

9 Understanding Homophones

❏ Read the directions and have students do the activity.

ANSWER KEY

1. feeds 2. degree 3. head 4. organs 5. subject
6. pick up 7. coin

UNDERSTANDING ITALICS AND QUOTATION MARKS

Italics

Write these examples on the board for each bullet point and explain:

■ Emphasis—*Most* dolphins can understand and follow hand signals.

■ Meaning—*Syntax* distinguishes language from general communication.

■ Title—The journal *Science* contains many interesting articles.

■ Foreign word—The *planum temporale* in both humans and chimps is the same size.

Quotation Marks

Write these examples on the board for each bullet point and explain:

■ Direct speech—When the chimp's kitten died, she signed, "Me sad."

■ Something different, not literal meaning—What are honeybees "saying" when they dance?

10 Understanding Italics and Quotations

❏ Read the directions.

❏ Give the students a time limit (15 minutes).

❏ If students finish early, have them check their answers with a partner.

ANSWER KEY

[B]

"smell messages"	something different
"home"	something different

[C]

"dance"	something different
"saying"	something different
"I want to play."	direct speech
"smiles"	something different

[D]

| "songs" | something different |

[E]

"talking"	something different
"say"	something different
"There's a tall blue human coming from the north."	direct speech

[F]

(*ball, basket, pipe*)	meaning
(*big, small, red*)	meaning
(*left, right*)	meaning
(*go, take*)	meaning
(*in, under*)	meaning
"Go to the ball on your right and take it to the basket."	direct speech

[H]

"take the potato outdoors"	direct speech
"go outdoors and get the potato"	direct speech
good, funny, hungry, stupid	meaning
"You me out."	direct speech
"Me banana you banana me you give."	direct speech
"water bird"	direct speech
"green banana"	direct speech
"Me sad."	direct speech

[I]

"Lana tomorrow scare snake river monster"	direct speech
planum temporale	foreign language
Science	title
"essentially identical"	direct speech

[J]

"Is it language?"	direct speech
syntax	meaning
"Some people think of language like pregnancy—you either have it or you don't."	direct speech
"a continuum of skills"	direct speech

11 **Finding Details**

Best Practice

Organizing Information

Activities such as this will teach students to organize information from a reading passage using a graphic organizer called a T-chart. This allows students to better assimilate and recall information at a later date, making it a valuable study tool. In this case, students identify examples of different types of animal communication mentioned in the passage.

❑ Direct students' attention to the T-chart. Ask them which animals use the types of communication listed in the first column.

❑ Tell them to work individually or in pairs to find information in the passage to fill in the second column. They can also do this assignment for homework.

ANSWER KEY

Answers may vary.

Types of Communication	Examples
smell	Smells have different meanings: to attract a mate, send a warning, mark a territory, or communicate where to find food.
body language	Body language can show directions to food or flowers, to express emotions or desires, or to demonstrate status.
vocalizations	Vocalizations can locate or identify objects or communicate with members of a group.
chatter (by prairie dogs)	Chatter can alert members of a group to danger or distinguish among creatures as to degree of danger.

symbols (used by dolphins)	Symbols like hand signals can be used to give commands to animals that they learn to follow.
symbols (used by primates)	Symbols like ASL and lexigrams can also be used for communication between chimps and humans.

12 **Checking your Vocabulary**

❑ Read the directions to the students.

❑ Divide them into small groups and tell them to work on the **Vocabulary Preview** taking turns and following the directions. You may want to give them a time limit (10–15 minutes) for this activity.

❑ Remind them that they should **not** use a dictionary—unless you think that it is appropriate at this point in the lesson.

❑ Discuss any vocabulary items with which the students are still having difficulty.

13 **Discussing the Reading**

Best Practice

Making Use of Academic Content

Activities such as this will help students extract meaning from context, a skill necessary for academic success. Although they may understand the main ideas in the reading passage about animal communication, they may not understand whether or not this communication can be considered "language." Taking notes on important details will help them develop this skill.

❑ Remind the students of the question from the last paragraph: Do animals simply communicate or do they really have a language?

❑ Ask the students to raise their hands if they think that the following animals have a language: bees and ants, dogs and cats, dolphins, prairie dogs, chimpanzees.

❑ Direct their attention to the charts in activity 1 and activity 2 and read the directions.

❑ Divide them into small groups and ask them to fill in the T-charts. Students' answers may differ from those listed here.

ANSWER KEY

Answers may vary.

1.

Communication	Language
Communication is the ability to use smell, body language, vocalizations, or symbols to relay messages to others of the same or different species.	Language is the ability to use vocalizations or symbols according to a set of rules, or *grammar*, that entails word order, or *syntax*. Mammals like dolphins and chimps may have a primitive ability to use language with training.

2.

Species	Capacity for language?	Evidence
prairie dogs	no	The chatter of prairie dogs seems to have as its main function to alert the colony to danger. Although they may be able to communicate 50 discrete meanings, we do not know if they use syntax.
dolphins	not sure	Although dolphins can understand and follow hand signals that have grammar and word order, they cannot, in turn, use these signals to communicate.
chimps	yes	Trained chimps can both understand and use ASL and lexigrams syntactically in short sentences and even coin new expressions when they don't know a word.

EXPANSION ACTIVITY

■ The aim of this activity is for students to think further about animal communication by making the sounds animals make in their language. It's also fun, but if students don't feel comfortable doing it, they can sit and watch.

■ Ask students from the same country to sit together in groups around the room.

■ Ask each group to make the sound of one of the animals listed in the book.

■ You might add other animals to the list, e.g., crow, sheep, goat, horse, camel, elephant, tiger, and so on.

■ Discuss reasons for differences.

"Parentese"

Before You Read

1 **Previewing the Topic**

- ❏ Have students read the questions and write brief answers.

- ❏ Put students into single-sex groups (i.e., women together and men together) to practice asking and answering questions. Give them a time limit (5–10 minutes) to finish the discussion.

- ❏ Call on students from each group to share their answer with the class.

2 **Identifying the Main Ideas**

- ❏ Write these languages on the board and underline the last syllable: *Chinese, Japanese, Vietnamese, Portuguese.* Ask who speaks these languages. Explain that the reading is about another language, *parentese*, and ask students to guess who speaks it.

- ❏ Read the directions and tell students to begin.

- ❏ Check the answers.

ANSWER KEY
A. (D) B. (B) C. (A) D. (A) E. (D)

Content Notes

- ■ Dr. Deborah Tannen is a professor of linguistics at Georgetown University in Washington, D.C. She has written many articles and books about gender differences in the speech of men and women.

- ■ Emory University in Atlanta, Georgia, promotes studies in cognition and development in the department of psychology. Professors and graduate students do research on how both child and adult listeners interpret the different intentions, thoughts, and feelings of speakers.

- ■ Dr. Campbell Leaper is a professor of psychology at the University of California at Santa Cruz. He has studied gender-related variations in parent-child speech.

After You Read

3 **Getting Meaning from Context**

- ❏ Read the directions.

- ❏ Remind students **not** to use a dictionary during this part of the lesson.

- ❏ Check the answers.

ANSWER KEY
Paragraph A
1. verbal
2. glue
Paragraph B
3. emotions
Paragraph C
4. realize
5. respond
6. apparently
Paragraph D
7. nature
8. nurture
9. evidence

4 Critical Thinking: Identifying Inferences

Best Practice

Cultivating Critical thinking

Activities such as this will help students identify inferences from statements in the reading. Even though they may think that some of the statements are true, they must consider them in the light of the reading to determine if they are inferences.

❑ Read the directions.

❑ Point out the answer in the first item.

❑ Tell the students to use highlighters to find the phrases in the reading, if possible.

❑ Then have the students check the statements where they have found the phrases from which they inferred the information and then write them on the lines.

❑ Check the answers when students are done.

ANSWER KEY

Answers may vary.

Paragraph A

1. ✓ *Most people believe that women talk more . . . but this is a stereotype.*

2. ✓ *. . . women are more verbal—talk more—in private situations/men talk more in public situations.*

Paragraph B

4. ✓ *There is also far more talk about emotion, especially sadness, with daughters than with sons.*

Paragraph C

5. ✓ *It is a known fact that at birth, males are a little less developed than females are. They don't vocalize . . . and they don't have as much eye contact. Female babies vocalize, look at their parents . . .*

Paragraph D

7. ✓ *A toy grocery store naturally involves more conversation.*

8. ✓ *A boy gets a car he can take apart and put back together again.*

Paragraph E

9. ✓ *Both boys and girls need "task-oriented" toys such as take-apart cars. With these toys, they practice the language that they will need, as adults, in work situations. Both boys and girls also need "social, interactive" toys such as a grocery store. With these toys, they practice the kind of conversation that is necessary in relationships with friends and family.*

Strategy

Distinguishing Facts from Assumptions

■ Write the "signal words" on the board:

FACT:	found proof	a known fact	evidence
ASSUMPTION:		believe	apparently
	suggest	seem	may/might

■ Call on a student to read the explanation from the **Strategy Box**.

5 Distinguishing Facts from Assumptions

- ❏ Read the directions and tell students to go back to the reading and underline the signal words for the fact or assumption.

- ❏ Then have the students write *fact* or *assumption* in the activity.

- ❏ Check answers.

ANSWER KEY

1. assumption: Most people **believe** that women talk more. [A]

2. fact: They **found evidence** that parents talk very differently . . . [B]

3. fact: It is **a known fact** that at birth . . . [C]

4. fact: . . . a study from UCSC **provides evidence** that . . . [D]

5. assumption: . . . Campbell Leaper . . . **believes** that the choice of toys is important. [E]

6. assumption: The **data suggest** that biology does not have to be . . . [E]

6 Discussing the Reading

- ❏ Direct the students' attention to the questions and read them.

- ❏ Divide students into small groups to discuss the answers and fill in the Venn diagram. Students' answers may differ from those listed here.

ANSWER KEY
Answers may vary.

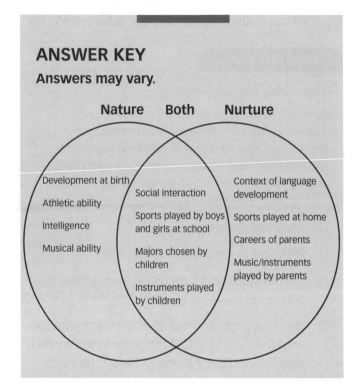

Nature | **Both** | **Nurture**

Nature:
- Development at birth
- Athletic ability
- Intelligence
- Musical ability

Both:
- Social interaction
- Sports played by boys and girls at school
- Majors chosen by children
- Instruments played by children

Nurture:
- Context of language development
- Sports played at home
- Careers of parents
- Music/Instruments played by parents

Responding in Writing

7 Summarizing

Best Practice

Scaffolding Instruction

Activities such as this will help students develop the ability to choose the main idea and important details of a paragraph in order to write a summary. By developing a model together, students are better equipped to write a summary independently later.

❑ Read the directions to the students. Write an outline of paragraph A on the board or on a transparency for an overhead projector (OHP):

Men and women—different styles of communication

> *Women—private situations = relationships*
>
> *Men—public situations = information, status*
>
> *Differences in childhood*
>
> > *girls—best friend > talking; verbal skills*
> >
> > *boys—groups > doing; mathematics*

❑ Write a summary of paragraph A on the board or a transparency:

> *Men and women have very different styles of communication. Generally, women talk more in private situations and use conversation to form relationships. Men talk more in public situations and use conversation to give information or show status. Actually, these differences begin in childhood when girls play with their best friends and develop verbal skills. Boys, on the other hand, play in groups in which they do rather than say things. As a result, girls are usually better at languages, while boys are better at math.*

❑ For variety, assign pairs of students a certain paragraph to outline and summarize.

❑ When students finish, have them compare their summary with those students who summarized the same paragraph.

8 Writing Your Own Ideas

❑ Read the directions to the students. You can assign the writing for homework or classwork.

❑ Be sure they identify the main idea of their paragraph.

Talk It Over

9 Toys

❑ For variety, visit a toy store nearby. Or bring in toy catalogs so students can cut out pictures and make posters in small groups that they can share with the class.

REPRODUCIBLE EXPANSION ACTIVITY

■ The aim of this activity is to further explore the theme of differences between male and female communication while children are playing.

■ Make a list of toy websites or use the ones below.

■ Check them before giving the assignment to students.

■ Photocopy and distribute **Black Line Master 20** "Toys for Girls and Boys" on page BLM20 of this Teacher's Edition.

■ Read the directions and the two examples.

■ Divide the students into small groups.

■ Give students a time limit (20–30 minutes) to do the activity. Alternatively, you can assign it for homework.

■ When students complete the worksheet, tell them to present their toys to the class.
> http://www.adventuretoys.co.uk/
> http://www.characterproducts.com/
> http://www.childtoystore.com/
> http://www.kbtoys.com/
> http://www.kidsurplus.com/toys.html
> http://www.mastermindtoys.com/
> http://www.toycentre.com/
> https://www.childcrafteducation.com/

1 Focusing on Words from the Academic Word List

❑ Direct students' attention to the list.

❑ Say the words and ask them to repeat, marking the stress on the appropriate syllable: *acquire'*, *capa'city*, *communica'tion*, *fo'cusing*, *iden'tical*, *jour'nal*, *re'search*, *struc'tures*, *percent'*.

❑ Ask students to repeat the list of words by themselves.

❑ Tell them to put the words in the sentences.

❑ When they finish, have them check their answers on page 147, paragraph I.

ANSWER KEY

1. communication 2. capacity 3. acquire
4. research 5. focusing 6. structures 7. journal
8. identical 9. capacity 10. percent

PREFIXES AND SUFFIXES

■ Direct students' attention to the list. Tell them you will read the prefixes and suffixes, and they will read the meanings aloud.

---

2 Working with Prefixes and Suffixes

❑ Read the directions. Call on a student to read the first example out loud.

❑ For variety, have students read in pairs or small groups.

❑ Tell them to begin the activity with their partners.

ANSWER KEY

1. converse (v) conversation (n) conversational (adj); conversation, converse, conversational

2. linguist (n) linguistic (adj) linguistics (n); linguistics, linguist, linguistic

3. reassurance (n) reassure (v) reassuringly (adv); reassure, reassurance, reassuringly

4. able (v) ability (n) ably (adv); ability, able, ably

5. appear (v) apparent (adj) apparently (adv); apparently, apparent, appear

6. simple (adj) simplify (v) simplified (adj); simplify, simplified, simple

7. vocal (adj) vocalize (v) vocalization (n); vocalize, vocal, vocalization

3 Understanding Words in Phrases

❑ Write these phrases on the board and tell students that they always go together in this order: *black and white*, *come and go*, *up and down*, *back and forth*.

❑ Tell them there are many other phrases that are commonly used together in academic writing.

❑ Read the directions and let them begin the activity.

ANSWER KEY

Paragraph A
1. together 2. gain 3. out 4. at
Paragraph B
5. light on
Paragraph C
6. known 7. eye 8. pay
Paragraph D
9. provide 10. apart/back together 11. on
Paragraph E
12. self-fulfilling

Strategy

Learning New Vocabulary: Making a Vocabulary Log

- On the board, copy the chart at the bottom of the **Strategy Box**. Explain the steps in making a Vocabulary Log.

- Write another word and elicit responses from the class: for example, *hybrid—a composite: The Toyota Prius is a <u>hybrid</u> car*.

4 Making a Vocabulary Log

- ❏ Tell students to choose five words from Chapters 1–7.

- ❏ Explain that using these five words, they should follow the steps from the **Strategy Box** to make their own Vocabulary Log.

- ❏ Tell students you will check their logs every week.

5 Searching the Internet

Best Practice

Activating Prior Knowledge

Activities such as this will enable students to link knowledge recently acquired with new information they gather from research. By working with partners, students will be able to think about what they have learned, add to it from what they encounter in their research, and share it with the rest of the class in a supportive environment.

- ❏ Divide students into pairs or small groups.

- ❏ Allow the groups to choose their topic. Instruct them to look at websites on the Internet; here are a few of them, but there are many more:

    Jane Goodall Institute
    http://www.janegoodall.org/

    Con Slobodchikoff
    http://www.prairiedog.info/Prairie_Dog_Communication.htm

    Louis Herman
    http://www.dolphin-institute.org/

    Deborah Tannen
    http://www.georgetown.edu/faculty/bassr/githens/tannen.htm

- ❏ Have the students present their findings to the class.

COMPREHENSION QUESTIONS ABOUT DETAILS

- Read the instructions in the box or call on two students to do so.

- Tell them that in tests such as the TOEFL® iBT, they won't be able to read the questions before they start. However, they will see the paragraph that contains the answer to each question after they skim the passage.

1 Practice

- ❑ Tell students to read the questions on page 166.

- ❑ Remind them to keep the questions in mind as they read the passage so they can mark the answers with a highlighter.

- ❑ Remind students **not** to use a dictionary during this part of the lesson.

- ❑ Give them a time limit (10 minutes).

- ❑ Check the answers.

ANSWER KEY

1. c 2. a 3. c 4. d 5. c 6. c

Content Notes

- Dr. Alan Firth was born and raised in England, but he got his Ph.D. and then became a professor at Aalborg University in northern Denmark. He has studied cross-cultural, business, and telecommunication interaction in English, and written numerous articles and books on those subjects.

- His Royal Highness, Prince Charles, the Prince of Wales, is heir apparent to the throne of the United Kingdom and the 15 Commonwealth Realms. He studied at Trinity College, Cambridge, and was the first member of the British Royal family to receive a degree. He also served in the British Royal Air Force and Royal Navy, as is the custom for male members of the royal family.

- Tom McArthur, an honorary fellow at the University of Exeter, wrote the *Oxford Companion to the English Language* and the *Oxford Guide to World English*. The latter book gives not only standard versions of British and American English, but also six geopolitical categories of English and its variations.

- The Australian government hosted the Cultural Diversity Conference in April, 1995, and well-known speakers from various sectors were invited to give papers. Dr. Braj Kachru, professor of linguistics at the University of Illinois, gave a talk titled the *International Nature of Modern English*, describing the *inner circle* of countries that speak it (USA—UK—Canada—Australia—New Zealand), the *outer circle* (Bangladesh—Ghana—India—Kenya—Malaysia—Nigeria—Pakistan—Philippines—Singapore—Sri Lanka—Tanzania—Zambia), and the *expanding circle* (China—Caribbean countries—Egypt—Indonesia—Israel—Japan—Korea—Nepal—Saudi Arabia—South Africa—South America—Taiwan—Commonwealth of Independent States [CIS]—Zimbabwe).

Beyond the Reading

2 Interviewing

- ❑ Read the directions.

- ❑ Students can choose to do one of these activities or the **Expansion Activity** with the Black Line Master, which is similar.

EXPANSION ACTIVITY

- The aim of this activity is to get students to think about the changes in the English language and the changes that are occurring in their own language because of the influence of English.

- Photocopy and distribute **Black Line Master 21** "Slang Expressions" on page BLM21 of this Teacher's Edition.

- Read the directions and do the first one together, writing the phrase on the board. If students have difficulty with Part I, do the rest with the class.

- Elicit an example for Part II (e.g., *biru* in Japanese is *beer* in English; *un parking* in Caribbean Spanish is *parking lot/garage*). Tell students to stand up and talk to others from their language group to finish the list, trying to think of a "pure" word from their language as a substitute.

- When students have completed the worksheet, have them put their words on the board in groups and present them to the class.

Self-Assessment Log

- ❏ Read the directions aloud and have students check vocabulary they learned in the chapter and are prepared to use.

- ❏ Have students check the strategies practiced in the chapter (or the degree to which they learned them). They have actually used all these strategies in Chapter 7.

- ❏ Put students in small groups. Ask students to find the information or an activity related to each strategy in the group.

- ❏ Tell students to find definitions in the chapter for any words they did not check.

8

Tastes and Preferences

In this chapter, students will read about the Silk Road and its history and significance in the first reading. They will also learn about the influence of religion on art and of the various civilizations that left their mark along the way of the caravans. In the second reading, students will learn about body art and the role it plays in the expression of cultural values and traditions. From clothing and decoration, to body and face paint, this form of art shows how ideal beauty among civilizations has differed through the ages.

Chapter Opener

❑ Direct students' attention to the photos on page 169 of the Student Book and ask questions: *What do you see in these pictures? How many of you live in or have visited this region of the world? What was the importance of the Silk Road in the past? What is its importance today?*

❑ Read the quotation and ask students what it means.

❑ Put these words on the board: *ancient travel routes, caravans, trade, archaeology*.

❑ Divide students into small groups and ask them to discuss these words. Have them generate a list of words that they associate with these concepts.

❑ Elicit some of these words from the students and write them on the board.

❝ Science and art belong to the whole world, and before them vanish the barriers of nationality. ❞

—Johann Wolfgang von Goethe
German philosopher and poet (1749–1832)

Chapter Overview

Reading Selections

The Silk Road: Art and Archaeology

Fashion: The Art of the Body

Reading Skills and Strategies

Previewing the topic and vocabulary

Previewing the reading

Getting meaning from context

Recognizing summaries in a reading

Skimming for main ideas

Critical Thinking Skills

Organizing information using an outline

Identifying and making inferences

Summarizing a paragraph

Vocabulary Building

Recognizing words with similar meanings

Understanding general and specific words

Understanding connotations

Focusing on the Academic Word List

Language Skills

Discussing ideas on art and beauty

Writing a paragraph

Focus on Testing TOEFL® IBT

Focusing on basic comprehension questions

Vocabulary

Nouns		Verbs	Adjectives	Prepositions	Expression
arabesques	mausoleums	called*	significant*	over*	to this end
archaeologists	merchants	depict	traditional*	under*	
architecture	mosques	flowered			
armor	oasis	founded*			
calligraphy	project*				
cosmetics	region*				
culture*	silk				
destination	statues				
documents*	technology*				
experts*					

*These words are from the Academic Word List. For more information on this list, see www.vuw.ac.nz/lals/research/awl.

The Silk Road: Art and Archaeology

Before You Read

1 Previewing the Topic

- ❑ Put students in small groups and have them discuss the questions.

- ❑ Call on students to share their answers with the class. Their answers may vary.

- ❑ Write on the board a few comments they may have about the discussion.

2 Previewing Vocabulary

- ❑ Read the directions to the students.

- ❑ Have them put a check (✓) next to the words they know.

- ❑ Tell them **not** to use a dictionary during this part of the lesson.

- ❑ Play the audio.

3 Previewing the Reading

- ❑ Read the questions and call on students to answer them.

- ❑ Comment on the answers, if necessary.

ANSWER KEY

Answers may vary.

1. Art and Archeology along the Silk road

2. Cross-Cultural Evidence; What Was the Silk Road?; Art, Religion, and the Silk Road; A Question of Time: Two Views; The Silk Road Today

3. The Silk Road was in Asia; many beautiful buildings, natural places, and artifacts can be found along the Silk Road.

Read

4 Reading the Article

- ❑ Read the directions.

- ❑ On the board write *What was the Silk Road? What can we learn about ancient life in this region from a study of the art and archaeology?* And ask students to think about this question as they are reading.

- ❑ Have students read the passage silently within a time limit (10–15 minutes) or have them follow along silently as you play the audio.

- ❑ Tell them to underline any words or phrases that are new or that they don't understand. Remind them **not** to use a dictionary during this part of the lesson.

- ❑ Play the audio.

Content Notes

- ■ c.e. = Common Era or Christian Era; 79 c.e. = 79 a.d.

- ■ b.c.e. = Before Common Era or Before Christian Era; 50 b.c.e. = 50 b.c.

After You Read

5 Checking Your Understanding

Best Practice

Making Use of Academic Content

Activities such as this will help expand students' ability to locate information in an academic text. With practice, they will learn to find answers to questions about a reading quickly and accurately and discuss it with peers.

- ❑ Read the directions.

- ❑ Put students in small groups and have them answer the questions within a time limit (10–15 minutes).

- ❑ Call on different students to give the answers.
- ❑ Discuss further if necessary.

ANSWER KEY

1. The three pieces of evidence were:

   - a mirror from India with an ivory handle in the shape of a fertility goddess, found in the Roman city of Pompeii, destroyed by a volcano in 79 c.e.;

   - a water pitcher in the shape of a vase combining different styles from Persia, Central Asia, and Greece, found in the tomb of Li Xian, a Chinese military official who died in 569 c.e.;

   - thousands of objects from Vietnam, western China, Iraq, the Roman Empire, and Egypt were found in the 8th century Shosoin Treasure House in Nara, Japan.

2. The opposite ends of the Silk Road were East Asia and the Mediterranean.

3. The goods whose method of production was kept a secret were Chinese silk and Mediterranean glass.

4. Merchants moved many goods such as spices, musical instruments, tea, valuable stones, wool, linen, and other fabrics. Ideas and knowledge were also moved along the Silk Road.

5. Merchants moved goods along the Silk Road using caravans.

6. The evidence of the movement of Buddhism to China is in the paintings and statues left behind; in Dunhuang, China, Buddhists dug a series of caves with frescoes depicting religious scenes and daily life.

7. Islamic art and architecture flowered along the Silk Road; in Samarkand, Timur built mosques, mausoleums, and palaces decorated with arabesques and Arabic calligraphy.

8. In the Takla Makan Desert in Central Asia, tall people were found in tombs; they dressed in brightly colored wool and wore leather boots;

they raised sheep and horses, used cowry shells for decoration, and ate bread, although wheat did not grow in that area.

9. Yo-Yo Ma's Silk Road Project encourages the preservation and spread of the living arts of these traditional lands.

6 Getting the Meaning from Context

- ❑ Read the directions. Remind students **not** to use a dictionary until they have completed this part of the lesson.

- ❑ Check the answers when students finish.

ANSWER KEY

1. verb/wall paintings/show, display

2. noun/built mosques/Islamic religious worship/ places of worship in Islamic religion, buildings for Islamic religious activities

Strategy

Getting Meaning from Context

- Write the two sentences in the **Example** on the board.

- Have two students read them.

- Ask which words in the sentences give clues to the meaning of *tombs*.

- Underline the words *died* and *people's bodies*.

- Tell students when they don't know the meaning of a word to use the strategy of looking at several contexts when possible.

7 Getting Meaning from Context

- ❑ Read the directions. Remind students **not** to use a dictionary until they have completed this part of the lesson.

- ❑ Check the answers when students finish.

ANSWER KEY

1. "rooms" inside mountains
2. religious, sacred
3. incredible, beautiful

8 Checking Your Vocabulary

- ❏ Read the directions.
- ❏ Put students in small groups and have them find the answers.
- ❏ Give students a time limit (10–15 minutes).
- ❏ Call on different students to give the answers.
- ❏ Discuss further if necessary.

ANSWER KEY

1. archaeologists 2. armor 3. silk 4. merchants 5. oasis 6. significant 7. documents 8. flowered 9. mausoleums 10. arabesques 11. calligraphy 12. destination 13. to this end

Strategy

Recognizing Summaries

- ■ Write the connecting words from the **Strategy Box** on the board.
- ■ Read the directions and say the words, asking students to repeat after you.

9 Recognizing Summaries

- ❏ Read the directions.
- ❏ Have the students look back at the reading to find the answers.
- ❏ Check the answers when students finish.

ANSWER KEY

1. *Clearly*, long before the globalization of our modern world, trade was going on between very distant lands, and the objects tell a story about a place and time.
2. *In short*, the Silk Road was the way that goods and ideas moved across a vast area of Asia and southeastern Europe.
3. *In brief*, it is possible to follow the rise and fall of religions by studying the art and architecture along the Silk Road.
4. *Thus*, archaeologists are beginning to ask, "Were people moving along the Silk Road long before we had thought?"
5. *The result is* that the people along the ancient Silk Road continue to learn from each other.

10 Understanding Outlines

Best Practice

Organizing Information

Activities such as this will teach students to organize information by filling in an outline. This allows them to identify main ideas and supporting details from sections of text and put them into a format that facilitates review at a later date.

- ❏ Read the directions.
- ❏ Tell students to do the activity using the outline and put the subtopics in the right place.

ANSWER KEY

The Silk Road: Art and Archaeology

I. Introduction: Cross-Cultural Evidence
   A. <u>example: Indian mirror in Roman Pompeii</u>
   B. <u>example: pitcher with styles from three cultures in a Chinese tomb</u>

C. <u>example: the Shosoin Treasure House in Japan</u>

D. *trade between distant lands long before today's globalization*

II. What Was the Silk Road?

A. <u>series or network of trails that connect East Asia to the Mediterranean</u>

1. <u>exchange of goods (silk, glass, spices, etc.)</u>

2. *exchange of ideas and knowledge*

B. <u>two Silk Roads</u>

1. <u>literal</u>

2. *figurative*

III. Art, Religion, and the Silk Road

A. <u>the spread of Buddhism north and east from India</u>

B. *the spread of Islam toward the east*

IV. A Question of Time: Two Views

A. <u>historical view</u>

1. *100 B.C.E.*

2. <u>General Zhang Qian, sent by emperor</u>

B. *archaeological view*

1. <u>1000 B.C.E.</u>

2. <u>tombs in the Takla Makan Desert</u>

V. The Silk Road Today

A. <u>new technology</u>

B. <u>tourism</u>

C. <u>encouragement of living arts</u>

11 Checking Your Understanding

Best Practice

Scaffolding Instruction

Activities such as this will allow students to better understand a reading by scaffolding instruction. The information that they have just learned about the Silk Road can be used as a scaffold upon which they can integrate new information found during research.

❑ Write the two questions on the board:

What was the Silk Road?

What can we learn about ancient life in this region from a study of the art and archaeology?

❑ Have a short class discussion, asking students to elaborate on answers.

REPRODUCIBLE   EXPANSION ACTIVITY

■ Photocopy and distribute **Black Line Master 22** "Traveling the Silk Road" on page BLM22 of this Teacher's Edition.

■ Tell students in pairs or small groups to choose a region or country along the Silk Road and one of the products from the area that was transported along it.

■ Keep a list to make sure that each one is different.

■ Have students look on the Internet for information about the topic.

■ Give them a few days to complete the assignment.

■ If time permits, have them look for pictures (or draw them) and make a poster for their presentation and display in the classroom.

■ When they finish, have them share their findings with the class.

12 Making Inferences

❑ Read the questions.

❑ Give the students five minutes to think about their answers to these questions.

❑ Call on different students to give the answers.

ANSWER KEY

1. Some were tall: a woman was 6 feet tall (1.83 meters), and a man 6 feet 6 inches (1.98 meters). Perhaps most astonishing, they had long noses and reddish hair, and the men wore beards.

2. People may have been traveling from Europe to Central Asia along the Silk Road as long ago as 1000 B.C.E. These people had characteristics of people from European countries rather than those from Asia.

13 Discussing the Reading

- ❑ Read the directions.

- ❑ Divide the students into small groups.

- ❑ Go around the room and listen to the discussion.

- ❑ Ask students to share their ideas with the class. (Answers will vary.)

Fashion: The Art of the Body

Before You Read

Strategy

Identifying Main Ideas by Analyzing Details

- Read the directions.

- Have a student read the paragraph in the example.

- Ask students what the different groups mentioned in the paragraph wear:

  the Inuit, nomadic desert people, the Indians of southern Chile, the tribal people of Australia.

- Ask students what the main idea is.

1   **Identifying Main Ideas by Analyzing Details**

- ❏ Read the directions.

- ❏ Remind students **not** to use a dictionary during this part of the lesson.

- ❏ Check the answers when students finish.

ANSWER KEY

[Paragraph A]   1. d   2. a, c, d   3. c
[Paragraph B]   1. d   2. a, b, d   3. b
[Paragraph C]   1. d   2. b, c   3. a
[Paragraph D]   1. c   2. b, c, d   3. b
[Paragraph E]   1. a   2. a, b, c   3. c

After You Read

2   **Critical Thinking: Identifying Inferences**

- ❏ Read the directions.

- ❏ Point out the answers in the first two examples.

- ❏ Tell the students to use highlighters to mark the phrases in the reading, if possible.

- ❏ Then have the students check the statements where they have found the phrases from which they inferred the information and then write them on the lines.

- ❏ Tell the students to work as quickly as possible.

- ❏ Check the answers when students finish.

ANSWER KEY

1. _X_ All people wear clothing to keep warm.

2. _✓_ Fur provides warmth, while long, loose clothing is useful in hot weather.

   The Inuit (Eskimos) wear animal fur to protect them against the cold winter weather. Nomadic desert people wear long, loose clothing for protection against the sun and wind of the Sahara.

3. _X_ Rich people wear more clothing than poor people do.

4. _✓_ Social status might be less important now than it was in the past.

   With the exception of the military, the divisions between different classes of society are becoming less clear. The clientele of a Paris café, for example, might include both working-class people and members of the highest society, but how can one tell the difference when everyone is wearing denim jeans?

5. _X_ Some methods of body beautification may be uncomfortable or painful.

6. _✓_ Body or face paint may make people feel protected.

   Anthropologists explain that it is a form of magic protection against the dangers of the world outside the village, where men have to go for the hunt or for war.

7. _X_ Women are more interested than men in looking good.

8. ✓ There are some similarities between tribal people and modern urban people in their views of body decoration.

In modern societies, however, cosmetics are used mostly by women, who often feel naked, unclothed, without makeup when out in public—like a tribal hunter without his warpaint.

3 Discussing the Reading

❑ Put students in small groups to discuss the questions.

❑ Call on some groups to share their answers with the class and discuss.

Responding in Writing

4 Summarizing

❑ Read the directions in the box. Tell students to choose one paragraph from paragraphs B, F, or G on pages 172–174.

❑ Give students a minute to decide which paragraph they will write about.

❑ Ask students who are going to summarize the same paragraph to sit together.

❑ Have them write a summary alone and then compare it to that of another student.

❑ When they have compared their summaries, collect and check them.

5 Writing Your Own Ideas

Best Practice

Activating Prior Knowledge

Activities such as summarizing a topic and expressing an opinion about it allow students to activate prior knowledge. This activity enables students to use their prior knowledge about society's views on these topics, formulate their own opinion, and express it in a letter to their teacher.

❑ Read the directions.

❑ Have students choose one of the topics listed and write you a letter for homework.

❑ Write this format on the board and tell students to copy it:

2/18/08

Dear _____,

> *I'd like to tell you my opinion of _____.*
> *In my country, many people think that*
> *_____ is _____. But I think that it is*
> *_____ because _____. In addition,*
> *_____. In short,*
> *_____ .*

> *Your student,*
> *Abdul*

❑ The next day, collect the letters.

❑ Pass them around to different students in the class. Make sure no one gets his or her own letter.

❑ Tell the students to read them and write the main idea of each letter at the bottom.

❑ Then have the students write a response to the letter on the back of the paper, telling their opinion on the topic.

❑ When students finish, they can give the letters back to the person who wrote them.

❑ After they have read them, collect and check them.

Talk It Over

6 Art and Beauty

❑ Read the directions.

❑ Divide students into small groups to discuss the questions about the quotations.

❑ Go around the room and listen to the discussions. Help the students with quotations they don't understand.

❑ Have them share their answers with the class.

7 **Analyzing Advertisements**

Best Practice

Cultivating Critical Thinking

Activities such as this allow students to engage in critical thinking as they consider the variety of beauty treatments available today. By doing research on the Internet and finding out how the treatment is done, by whom, and to whom, they will be better able to evaluate its worth and formulate an opinion about it.

❑ Ask students what kinds of beauty treatments are available to people today.

❑ Make a list on the board, dividing the treatments into categories, such as hair, skin, nails, body-building/slimming, injections (Botox, collagen), cosmetic surgery, and so on.

❑ Tell students to choose one of these categories to research and present to the class.

 EXPANSION ACTIVITY
REPRODUCIBLE

■ Photocopy and distribute **Black Line Master 23** "Beauty Treatments" on page BLM23 of this Teacher's Edition.

■ Allow students to choose a type of beauty treatment in pairs or small groups.

■ Have them go to the computer lab or do the activity at home.

■ Give them a few days to finish the assignment.

■ Tell students to make a poster or PowerPoint presentation of their research.

■ Have them present their findings to the class.

Strategy

Recognizing Words with Similar Meanings

- Write the **Examples** from the **Strategy Box** on the board.

- Ask a student to read them.

- Elicit the meanings of the words (*course*, *class*, *lesson*) from the students, or read them to the students.

1   **Recognizing Words with Similar Meanings**

- ❑ Read the directions.

- ❑ Ask students to do the activity quickly.

- ❑ Check the answers with the class.

ANSWER KEY

1. b, c, a   2. a, b, c   3. c, a, b

Strategy

Understanding General and Specific Words

- Put the **Example** on the board:

   Beautiful art can be found in different kinds of structures: churches, mosques, and palaces.

- Underline the general word, *structures*, and the specific words, *churches*, *mosques*, and *palaces*.

- Ask students which word is general, and which words are specific.

- Tell them that the general word is the *category* that the particular words belong to.

2   **Understanding General and Specific Words**

- ❑ Read the directions.

- ❑ Ask students to do the activity quickly.

- ❑ Check the answers with the class.

ANSWER KEY

1. art   2. writing   3. architecture   4. traveler
5. transportation   6. cosmetics   7. religion   8. crime

Strategy

Understanding Connotations

- Write the **Examples** from the Strategy Box on the board.

- Ask a student to read them.

- Elicit the meanings of the words (*plump*, *large*, *fat*) from the students, or read them to the students.

3   **Understanding Connotations**

- ❑ Read the directions.

- ❑ Have students work on the activity in pairs.

- ❑ Check the answers when finished.

ANSWER KEY

1. +   2. –   3. –   4. +   5. –   6. –
③ plump ④ chubby

1. beautiful   2. hideous   3. beautiful   4. ugly
5. beautiful   6. ugly

4   **Choosing the Appropriate Words**

- ❑ Read the directions.

- ❑ Have students work on the activity in pairs.

- ❑ Check the answers when finished.

ANSWER KEY

1. b, c 2. a, c 3. c, d

5 Writing Words with Similar Meanings

Best Practice

Interacting with Others

Activities such as this will encourage students to expand their basic vocabulary and add variety to their speaking and writing. Making lists of words with similar meanings, or synonyms, on the board with other students will increase the range of their vocabulary and help them on the TOEFL® iBT.

❑ Read the directions.

❑ Have students work on the activity in pairs.

❑ Tell them to make lists of synonyms on the board.

❑ Discuss the differences in meaning, connotation, and usage with the class.

ANSWER KEY

Answers may vary.

1. adult female, mother 2. robber, burglar
3. speak, discuss, converse 4. think, know, hope
5. ancient, elderly, worn 6. tiny, petite, minuscule

6 Recognizing Words in Phrases

❑ Read the directions.

❑ Tell students to guess the words before they look them up.

❑ Have them check their answers with the reading.

[A] in the shape of . . .
[B] a network of . . .
[C] was used from . . . to . . .

[D] from . . . to . . .
[E] a desert oasis
[F] 1. contributed to; 2. In brief . . .
[H] To this end . . .

7 Focusing on Words from the Academic Word List

❑ Read the directions.

❑ Tell students to guess the words before they look them up.

❑ Have them check their answers with the reading on pages 174–175.

ANSWER KEY

1. culture 2. called 3. technology 4. under
5. over 6. routes 7. experts 8. region 9. founded
10. project 11. traditional

8 Searching the Internet

❑ Read the directions.

❑ Tell students to choose one of the topics.

❑ Divide the students into pairs or small groups according to the topic they have chosen.

❑ Tell them to find a website and prepare a short report.

❑ Have each person write, draw, or upload images for the presentation (PowerPoint, poster, drawings on board).

❑ Have them share their findings with the class.

QUESTIONS ABOUT BASIC COMPREHENSION

- Put the three types of questions from **Chapter 1** on the board:

    Information questions—scanning for words or numbers

    Basic comprehension questions—vocabulary, grammar, organization of passage

    Reading to learn—main ideas, implied ideas, author's attitudes, relations among facts

- Explain the types of questions and read the paragraph in the box to students.

- Tell the students that they will do an activity that will help prepare them for the iBT.

---

1 Practice

- Read the directions, telling students to skim the reading on pages 164–165 of Chapter 7 in 5 minutes, as they have already read it before. Write the beginning and ending time on the board (e.g., 10:45–10:50).

- When time is up, tell them to do the questions in 5 minutes, and write the beginning and ending time on the board.

- Check the answers when students finish.

ANSWER KEY

1. a 2. c 3. a 4. b 5. c

Self-Assessment Log

- ❑ Read the directions aloud and have students check vocabulary they learned in the chapter and are prepared to use.

- ❑ Have students check the strategies practiced in the chapter (or the degree to which they learned them). They have actually used all these strategies in Chapter 8.

- ❑ Put students in small groups. Ask students to find the information or an activity related to each strategy in the group.

- ❑ Tell students to find definitions in the chapter for any words they did not check.

REPRODUCIBLE **EXPANSION ACTIVITY**

- Photocopy and distribute **Black Line Master 24** "Spelling and Synonyms" on page BLM24 of this Teacher's Edition.

- Read the directions.

- Dictate the words from the **Target Vocabulary List** to the students if time is limited. Or write each word on a slip of paper and divide the slips among the students.

- Have each student say the word on the slip loudly and clearly to the class.

- Students write down 15 words on the **Black Line Master**.

- When all the words have been said, tell the students to write a synonym or meaning beside the word without using a dictionary.

- Have students check their own papers by looking at the **Target Vocabulary List** on page 195.

- When they finish, elicit synonyms or meanings. Students can use this sheet to study for the **Chapter Test**.

9

New Frontiers

In this chapter, students will read about the different parts of the brain and their functions. They will also learn about the teen brain, differences between male and female brains, and activities that can either damage or enhance the functioning of the brain. In the second reading, students will read about the familiar nature versus nurture controversy. Twin studies, genetics, and chemicals that stimulate or suppress the brain will also be explored in this regard.

Chapter Opener

❏ Direct students' attention to the photo on page 197 of the Student Book and ask them what they know about the human brain.

❏ Read the quotation and ask students what it means. Ask them if they know anything about Lyall Watson, and then tell them some information about him.

❝ If the brain were so simple [that] we could understand it, we would be so simple [that] we couldn't. ❞

—Lyall Watson
Africa-born biologist and writer, (1939–)

Chapter Overview

Reading Selections

The Human Brain—New Discoveries

Personality: Nature or Nurture?

Reading Skills and Strategies

Previewing the topic and vocabulary

Previewing the reading

Predicting content of a reading

Identifying the main ideas

Skimming for main ideas

Critical Thinking Skills

Analyzing diagrams and photographs

Distinguishing facts from assumptions

Synthesizing and applying information from a reading

Categorizing

Making inferences

Summarizing a paragraph

Vocabulary Building

Matching words with similar meanings

Putting words into categories

Analyzing word roots and affixes

Focusing on the Academic Word List

Language Skills

Expressing opinions based on facts

Identifying similarities and differences among family members

Writing a paragraph

Focus on Testing TOEFL® IBT

Getting meaning from context

Vocabulary

Nouns		Verb	Adjectives
aduts*	logic*	imply*	involved*
colleagues*	maturation*		mature*
evidence*	maturity*		mental*
identity*	memory		
infant	neuroscientists		
insights*	personality		
institute*	psychologist*		
intelligence*	researchers*		

*These words are from the Academic Word List. For more information on this list, see www.vuw.ac.nz/lals/research/awl.

The Human Brain—New Discoveries

Before You Read

1 Getting Started

> **Best Practice**
>
> **Scaffolding Instruction**
>
> Activities such as this will allow students to better understand a reading by scaffolding instruction. The information that they have just learned from the drawing can be used as a scaffold upon which they can integrate new information from the reading.

- ❑ Direct students' attention to the drawing and have students say the name of each part of the brain after you. Ask them to read the captions about the brain.

- ❑ Put students in small groups and have them discuss the questions.

- ❑ Call on students to share their answers with the class. Their answers may vary.

- ❑ Write on the board a few of their comments.

ANSWER KEY
Answers may vary.

1. Compose music—cerebrum, cortex, temporal lobe, frontal lobe; throw a ball—cerebellum, occipital lobe, parietal lobe, frontal lobe; paint a picture—cerebrum, cortex, occipital lobe, parietal lobe, frontal lobe, cerebellum.
2. Cold—hypothalamus, cerebrum, cortex
3. Man in photo B because he's with his friends
4. It's typical for both girls and boys to play sports and tell secrets.
5. Men/women—corpus callosum, hypothalamus

2 Previewing the Reading

- ❑ Read the questions and call on students to answer them.

- ❑ Comment on the answers, if necessary.

ANSWER KEY

1. The Human Brain—New Discoveries
2. Parts of the Brain; Left Brain/Right Brain: Creativity; Memory—True or False?; The Teen Brain; Differences in Male and Female Brains; Hypothalamus; A Change of Mind?; Meditation
3. Answers may vary.

3 Preparing to Read

- ❑ Read the directions.

- ❑ Call on different students to read each question.

- ❑ Ask class if they think the reading will answer that question.

- ❑ Comment on the answers, if necessary.

ANSWER KEY
Answers may vary.

1. ✓ 2. ✓ 3. ✓ 4. ✓ 5. – 6. ✓ 7. ✓ 8. ✓ 9. –
10. ✓ 11. –

4 Previewing Vocabulary

- ❑ Read the directions to the students.

- ❑ Have them put a check (✓) next to the words they know.

- ❑ Tell them **not** to use a dictionary during this part of the lesson.

- ❑ Play the audio.

Read

5 Reading an Article

- ❏ Read the directions.

- ❏ Have students read the passage silently within a time limit (10–15 minutes) or have them follow along silently as you play the audio.

- ❏ Tell them to underline any words or phrases that are new or that they don't understand. Remind them **not** to use a dictionary during this part of the lesson.

- ❏ Play the audio.

After You Read

6 Getting the Main Ideas

- ❏ Read the directions.

- ❏ Have students work on the activity individually.

- ❏ Call on different students to read the statements and give the answers.

- ❏ Discuss further if necessary.

ANSWER KEY

1. T 2. T 3. F 4. F 5. F 6. T

7 Vocabulary Check

- ❏ Read the directions.

- ❏ Put students in pairs and remind them **not** to use a dictionary until they have completed this part of the lesson.

- ❏ Discuss the answers when students finish.

Strategy

Distinguishing Facts from Assumptions

- ■ Write these words on the board:

    FACT information proven to be true

    ASSUMPTION ideas believed but not proven to be true

- ■ Read the directions for the first part and tell the class to repeat the words after you and say the parts of speech:

certain adj.	objective adj.	scientific adj.
clear adj.	positive adj.	show v.
know v.	prove v.	sure adj.

- ■ Read the directions for the second part and tell the class to repeat the words after you and say the parts of speech:

claim v.	imply v.
possibly adv.	
(dis)agree v.	likely adj.
probably adv.	theorize v.
doubt v.	possible adj.
subjective adj.	think v.

8 Distinguishing Facts from Assumptions

- ❏ Read the directions.

- ❏ Tell students to do the activity in pairs.

- ❏ Check the answers when students finish.

ANSWER KEY

1. **fact**—*Psychologists agree that most of us have creative ability that is greater than what we use in daily life.*

2. **assumption**—*Therefore, many of us might not "exercise" our right hemisphere much, except through dreams, symbols, and those wonderful insights in which we suddenly find the answer to a problem that has been bothering us.*

3. **assumption**—*Can we be taught to use our right hemisphere more? Many experts believe so.*

4. **assumption**—*Classes at some schools and books (such as* The Inner Game of Tennis *and* Drawing on the Right Side of the Brain*) claim to help people "silence" the left hemisphere and give the right a chance to work.*

5. **fact**—*In fact, over 700 cases have been filed that are based on these repressed memories.*

6. **assumption**—*However, studies in the 1990s suggested that many of these might be false memories.*

7. **fact**—*It is known that small pieces of a memory (sound, sight, feeling, and so on) are kept in different parts of the brain; the limbic system, in the middle of the brain, pulls these pieces together into one complete memory.*

8. **fact**—*But it's certain that people can "remember" things that have never happened.*

9. **assumption**—*Most frightening, according to Dr. Michael Nash of the University of Tennessee, is that "there may be no structural difference" in the brain between a false memory and a true one.*

10. **fact**—*However, very recent studies provide evidence that the brain of a teenager differs from that of both children and adults.*

11. **assumption**—*Because, it is believed, the corpus callosum is involved in self-awareness and intelligence, the new studies imply that teens may not be as fully self-aware or as intelligent as they will be later.*

12. **fact**—*One recent study shows that there is a region in the hypothalamus that is larger in heterosexual men than it is in women and homosexual men.*

13. **assumption**—*The corpus callosum is larger in women than in men. This might explain the mystery of "female intuition," which is supposed to give women greater ability to "read" and understand emotional clues.*

14. **fact**—*a study from the University of Aberdeen and the University of Edinburgh, in England concludes that smoking makes people less intelligent.*

15. **assumption**—*meditation seems to change the "wiring" in the brain in several positive ways.*

9 **Checking Your Understanding**

Best Practice

Making Use of Academic Content

Activities such as this will help expand students' ability to locate information in an academic text. With practice, they will learn to find answers to questions about a reading quickly and accurately.

❑ Read the directions.

❑ Tell students to do the activity in pairs. Give them a time limit (10–15 minutes).

❑ Call on different students to read the questions and answers.

❑ Discuss further if necessary.

ANSWER KEY

Answers may vary.

1. Different parts of the brain are responsible for different functions of the body.

2. Animal brains have a subcortex, which is responsible for basic functions whereas human brains have the neocortex, which is where complex activities take place.

3. Some people use the right hemisphere more than others do.

4. The left side of the brain is where reading, writing, and mathematics are processed; the right side is where music, art, dreams, symbols, and insights are processed.

5. Not answered in the reading.

6. Yes, because small pieces of memory are kept in different parts of the brain, and the limbic system pulls these pieces together into one complete memory, making it possible to have a false one.

7. Meditation can improve our memories.

8. In teenagers' brains, the corpus callosum continues to grow, so the self-awareness and intelligence of young people are still developing.

9. Not answered in the reading.

10. Smoking and "infomania" can reduce intelligence.

11. Not answered in the reading.

10 Critical Thinking: Application

❏ Read the directions.

❏ Put students in small groups.

❏ Go around the room and comment on lists, if necessary.

❏ Ask students to share their lists with the class.

EXPANSION ACTIVITY

REPRODUCIBLE

■ The aim of this activity is to encourage students to apply what they have learned in the reading to their own experience.

■ Photocopy and distribute **Black Line Master 25** "Improving Your Brain" on page BLM25 of this Teacher's Edition.

■ Put students in pairs or small groups to review paragraphs [H] and [I] and list things that are good and bad for the brain.

■ Tell them to search the Internet and look for more ideas.

■ Point out to students that they should also list how they plan to improve the functioning of their own brains.

■ Give them a few days to complete the assignment.

■ When they finish, have them share their findings with the class.

Personality: Nature or Nurture?

Before You Read

1   **Identifying the Main Idea by Analyzing Details**

❏   Read the directions.

❏   Remind students **not** to use a dictionary during this part of the lesson.

❏   Have students read the passage silently within a time limit (10–15 minutes) or have them follow along silently as you play the audio.

❏   Check the answers when students finish.

ANSWER KEY

[A]   1. d   2. b, c, d, e
     3. both nature and nurture play a role in determining a person's identity

[B]   1. c   2. b, c, e
     3. genetics (nature/biology) plays a significant role in determining personal characteristics and behavior

[C]   1. e   2. a, b, c, e
     3. a surprising number of traits are heritable, or due to nature

[D]   1. b   2. a, c, d, e
     3. genes work together with the chemicals in the body to influence personality

[E]   1. a   2. a, b, d, e
     3. although personality traits are largely heritable, the environment still plays an important role in their development

After You Read

2   **Critical Thinking: Making Inferences**

❏   Read the directions.

❏   Tell the students to work as quickly as possible.

❏   Check the answers when students finish.

ANSWER KEY

1.   ✓   The philosophical question of nature/nurture is an old one.

    The nature/nurture question is not a new one.

2.   X   The environment in which Jim Springer and Jim Lewis grew up had no effect on their behavior or personality.

3.   ✓   The goal of twin studies is to identify the amount of influence from genes and the amount from education and experiences that determine our identity.

    Today, we realize that both play a role. The question now is, to what degree? To answer this question, researchers are studying identical twins, especially those who grew up in different environments.

    Various research centers are studying identical twins in order to discover the "heritablility" of behavioral characteristics—that is, the degree to which a trait is due to genes ("nature") instead of environment.

4.   ✓   Our possibility of being happy is mostly a result of our genes, not our situation in life.

    Another study tells us that happiness does not depend much on money or love or professional success; instead, it is 80 percent heritable!

5.   X   A single gene determines each personality characteristic.

6.   ✓   The genetic contribution to personality is complicated.

    However, one gene alone cannot cause people to become anxious or homosexual or thrill seeking. Instead, many genes work together, and they direct the combination of chemicals in the body.

7.   X   Human beings are able to change their genetics.

3 Discussing the Reading

- ❑ Read the directions.

- ❑ Put students in small groups to discuss questions.

- ❑ Go around the room and comment on answers, if necessary.

Responding in Writing

4 **Summarizing**

- ❑ Read the directions.

- ❑ Give students a minute to decide which part they will write about.

- ❑ Ask students who are going to summarize the same paragraph to sit together.

- ❑ Have them write a summary alone and then compare it to that of one of the other students who is summarizing the same paragraph.

- ❑ When they have compared their summaries, collect and check them.

5 **Writing Your Own Ideas**

Best Practice

Activating Prior Knowledge

Activities such as applying a concept from a reading to their personal experience will help students understand it better. Writing a letter to a family member will enable them to explore a topic and perhaps come to a better understanding of it.

- ❑ Read the directions.

- ❑ Have students choose one of the topics listed and write you a letter for homework.

- ❑ Write this format on the board and tell students to copy it:

4/25/07

Dear _____ ,

I remember when we used to talk about the vacation we spent in Ibiza when we were little. You said we stayed at a small hotel, but I remember that we camped out on the beach. We fished and ate what we caught, but you remember eating in country restaurants on the hillsides. We had a lot of fun on that vacation, but why do we each remember it so differently?

Your sister,

Anna

- ❑ The next day, collect the letters.

- ❑ Pass them around to different students in the class. Make sure no one gets his or her own letter.

- ❑ Tell the students to read them and write the main idea of each letter at the bottom.

- ❑ Then have the students write a response to the letter on the back of the paper, telling their opinion on the topic.

- ❑ When students finish, they can give the letters back to the person who wrote them.

- ❑ After they have read them, collect and check them.

Talk it Over

6 **Genes for Crime?**

Best Practice

Cultivating Critical Thinking

Activities such as this allow students to engage in critical thinking as they consider the possibility of the existence of a genetic link to violence or criminality. By doing research on the Internet and investigating the details, they will be better able to evaluate the possibility and form an opinion about it.

- Have two students read the two paragraphs.

- Ask students what they think.

- Tell them they will research the topic in the next activity.

EXPANSION ACTIVITY

- The aim of this activity is to engage the students in critical thinking about a topic related to the reading.

- Photocopy and distribute **Black Line Master 26** "Violence and Genetics" on page BLM26 of this Teacher's Edition.

- Tell students to outline the article according to the sections on the **Black Line Master**, if possible. They can also make up different sections.

- Have students go to the computer lab or do the activity at home.

- Give them a few days to finish the assignment.

- Allow students to choose sides on this issue after they do research and hold a debate.

- Have them present their findings to the class.

1 Understanding Words with Similar Meanings

- ❑ Read the directions.
- ❑ Ask students to do the activity quickly.
- ❑ Check the answers with the class.

ANSWER KEY
1. c, a, b 2. b, a, c 3. c, b, a 4. c, a, b

Strategy

Putting Words in Categories

- ▪ Write the words from the **Example** in the **Strategy Box** on the board:

  laboratory, neuroscientist, subjects, experiment

- ▪ Ask a student to read them.
- ▪ Elicit the content area from the students (*science*).
- ▪ Read the explanation.

2 Putting Words in Categories

Best Practice

Organizing Information
Activities such as this will teach students to organize words into categories or content areas. This will help them in both reading and writing to recognize and use synonyms, distinguishing between slight differences in meaning.

- ❑ Read the directions.
- ❑ Have students work on the activity as a class.
- ❑ Check the answers when finished.

ANSWER KEY
1. ~~nurture~~ / genetics 2. ~~maturity~~ / young child
3. ~~musician~~ / medical/health 4. ~~creativity~~ / parts of the brain 5. ~~meditation~~ / illness, disorder, condition 6. ~~anxiety~~ / physical characteristics
7. ~~dreams~~ / subjects

ANALYZING WORD ROOTS AND AFFIXES

- ▪ Read the directions.
- ▪ Read the **Affixes** and ask students to read the **Meanings**.

3 Analyzing Word Roots and Affixes

- ❑ Read the directions.
- ❑ Have students do the activity quickly.
- ❑ Check the answers.

ANSWER KEY
1. c 2. a 3. d 4. b 5. e 6. d 7. a 8. d

4 Focusing on Words from the Academic Word List

- ❑ Read the directions.
- ❑ Have students do the activity quickly.
- ❑ Check the answers.

ANSWER KEY
1. traditional 2. mature 3. evidence 4. Institute
5. Mental 6. maturation 7. colleagues
8. involved 9. intelligence 10. imply
11. intelligent 12. researchers 13. adults

5 Searching the Internet

Best Practice

Interacting with Others

Activities such as this will encourage students to explore a topic of interest with their peers. They will develop the skills of working together to find information and organizing it in a logical way to present it to the class.

EXPANSION ACTIVITY

- The purpose of this activity is to encourage students to do research on topics presented in the readings.

- Allow them to choose a topic and search the Internet with others who have chosen the same one.

- Have them prepare a poster or an outline on the board and present their topic to the class.

- Remind students that each one in the group must speak during the presentation.

- Have the other students write down one or two questions to ask the group after their presentation.

TOEFL® IBT

GETTING MEANING FROM CONTEXT

- Put these hints on the board:

  A word can be defined or explained in

  same → | sentence
  previous → | *or*
  following → | a different paragraph

- Use the context to figure it out.

- Tell the students that the **Practice** will help prepare them for the iBT.

1 Practice

- ❑ Read the directions, telling students to do the activity quickly. Write a beginning and ending time on the board (10–15 minutes).

- ❑ When time is up, tell them to stop working.

- ❑ Check the answers when students finish.

ANSWER KEY

1. c 2. d 3. b 4. c 5. d 6. c 7. a

Self-Assessment Log

- ❑ Read the directions aloud and have students check vocabulary they learned in the chapter and are prepared to use.

- ❑ Have students check the strategies practiced in the chapter (or the degree to which they learned them). They have actually used all these strategies in Chapter 9.

- ❑ Put students in small groups. Ask students to find the information or an activity related to each strategy in the group.

- ❑ Tell students to find definitions in the chapter for any words they did not check.

EXPANSION ACTIVITY

- The aim of this activity is to have students practice the parts of speech of words in the **Target Vocabulary**.

- Photocopy and distribute **Black Line Master 27** "Parts of Speech" on page BLM27 of this Teacher's Edition.

- Read the directions.

- Tell students to work individually and then in pairs.

- Have students check their work using a dictionary.

10

Ceremonies

In this chapter, students will read about the different rites of passage and what they signify. Among the rites they will learn about are the passage to adulthood among Native Americans, the birth of a baby in Korea, Islamic weddings, and funerals in Thailand. They will also read a passage describing how some of these traditional rituals are changing as people seek to adopt those of other cultures. Finally, they will read about learning to drive in the United States, a rite of passage from adolescence to adulthood.

Chapter Opener

❏ Direct students' attention to the photo on page 219 of the Student Book and ask students what they know about rites of passage.

❏ Read the quotation and ask students what it means. Ask them what they know about Sun Bear, and tell them a little about his life. See information below.

❝ When humans participate in ceremony, they enter a sacred space. Everything outside of that space shrivels in importance. Time takes on a different dimension. **❞**

—Sun Bear
Medicine Chief of the Bear Tribe Medicine Society (1929–1992)

Chapter Overview

Reading Selections

Rites of Passage

New Days, New Ways: Changing Rites of Passage

Reading Skills and Strategies

Previewing the reading

Previewing the topic and vocabulary

Identifying the main ideas and writing summaries of each paragraph in a reading

Understanding chronology: scanning for time words

Understanding symbols

Critical Thinking Skills

Making inferences

Comparing and contrasting

Using a graphic organizer to organize and analyze information

Distinguishing facts from opinions

Summarizing a paragraph

Vocabulary Building

Determining categories

Analyzing word roots and affixes

Focusing on the Academic Word List

Language Skills

Applying information in the reading to personal situation

Conducting a survey on traditional and nontraditional weddings

Writing a paragraph

Focus on Testing TOEFL® iBT

Identifying main idea patterns

Vocabulary

Nouns	Verbs	Adjectives	Adverb
coffin	chant	indigenous	physically*
community*	wail	previous*	
cremation			
deceased			
funerals			
incorporation*			
monks			
rite of passage			
status*			
transition*			
trousseau			
vision*			

*These words are from the Academic Word List. For more information on this list, see www.vuw.ac.nz/lals/research/awl.

Rites of Passage

Before You Read

1 Getting Started

- ❑ Direct students' attention to the questions.
- ❑ Put students in small groups and have them discuss the questions.
- ❑ Call on students to share their answers with the class. Their answers may vary.
- ❑ Write on the board a few comments they may have about the discussion.

2 Previewing the Reading

- ❑ Have the students quickly look over the photos and reading.
- ❑ Read the questions and call on students to answer them.
- ❑ Comment on the answers, if necessary.

ANSWER KEY

1. Rights of Passage—What Are Rites of Passage?; Birth Rituals in Korea; Islamic Weddings; Funerals in Thailand; The Timelessness of Rites of Passage

2. Answers will vary.

3. Questions will vary.

3 Previewing Vocabulary

- ❑ Read the directions to the students.
- ❑ Have them put a check mark (✓) next to the words they know.
- ❑ Tell them **not** to use a dictionary during this part of the lesson.
- ❑ Play the audio.

Read

4 Reading an Article

- ❑ Read the directions.
- ❑ Have students read the passage silently within a time limit (10–15 minutes) or have them follow along silently as you play the audio.
- ❑ Tell them to think about the questions they wrote for Activity 2.
- ❑ Tell them to underline any words or phrases that are new or that they don't understand. Remind them **not** to use a dictionary during this part of the lesson.
- ❑ Play the audio.

After You Read

5 Getting the Main Ideas

Best Practice

Organizing Information

Activities such as this will teach students to organize ideas chronologically into steps in a process. This will help them to recognize these steps when reading and set them out in an organized way when writing.

- ❑ Read the directions and look at the example of the first answer in the chart.
- ❑ Have students work on the activity individually.
- ❑ Call on different students to read the statements and give the answers.
- ❑ Discuss further, if necessary.

ANSWER KEY

Answers may vary.

Rite of Passage	Previous Status	Transition	New Status
vision quest	a boy	4 days isolated in a cave, not a boy or a man	a man with an adult name
birth rituals	pregnant women don't eat certain foods; doors are left open	the baby is born	mother drinks seaweed soup; no cold water for 21 days; 100-day ceremony to become member of community
Islamic wedding	two separate families	ask for hand, marriage contract, henna party, sword dance, trousseau, guests with gifts	married couple; bride comfortable in new home
Buddhist funeral	dying person listening to scriptures	death, chanting, body washed, put in coffin, cremation, music and company for comfort	spirit cut off from world and person is reborn in a new body

6 **Checking Vocabulary**

❑ Read the directions.

❑ Put students in pairs and remind them **not** to use a dictionary until they have completed this part of the lesson.

❑ Discuss the answers when students finish.

7 **Making Inferences**

❑ Read the directions.

❑ Put students in pairs and remind them **not** to use a dictionary until they have completed this part of the lesson.

❑ Discuss the answers when students finish.

ANSWER KEY

1. _✓_ In a vision quest, a boy finds out about his future career from his vision.

   At the end, when he comes out of the cave, he is a man, with an adult name, and he knows what his livelihood will be.

2. _✓_ Korean parents might put a soccer ball in front of their one-year-old if they want him or her to be a great soccer player.

   These days, people can add any object, such as a baseball, if they want their child to be a great baseball player.

3. ____ The Bedouin marriage contract involves money.

4. ____ People who put objects in the graves of the dead may have religious beliefs.

UNDERSTANDING CHRONOLOGY

- Direct students' attention to the words in the box.

- Ask them which words they would expect to find at the beginning, middle, and end of a paragraph.

- As the students say the words, put them on the board. Explain that *chronology* means the order in which events happen.

Beginning	Middle		End
first	after	after that	last
beginning	next	the next step	finally
second	then	at this point	

8 Understanding Chronology

- ❑ Read the directions.
- ❑ Tell students to do the activity in pairs.
- ❑ Check the answers when students finish.

ANSWER KEY

1.3 2.5 3.1 4.4 5.2

UNDERSTANDING SYMBOLS

- Direct students' attention to the box.

- Write the word *SYMBOL* on the board.

- If there are any symbols in the classroom (baseball caps with logos, an item with the name of a school, city, or sports team) point them out and ask students what each one represents.

- Read the explanation.

- Say the words and have students repeat them after you.

9 Understanding Symbols

- ❑ Read the directions.
- ❑ Tell students to do the activity in pairs.

ANSWER KEY

1. *The belief is that the smoke from the pipe goes up to the spirit world and allows power to come down.*

2. *Family members leave doors open, and do not repair rooms, doors, or fireplaces in the kitchen. All these symbolize an easy delivery.*

3. *The henna is more than just skin paint. It is associated with health, beauty, and luck.*

10 Checking Your Understanding

- ❑ Read the directions.
- ❑ Tell students to do the activity in pairs.
- ❑ Call on different students to read their questions and answers.
- ❑ Discuss further if necessary.

ANSWER KEY

Answers will vary.

11 Applying the Reading

- ❑ Read the directions.
- ❑ Put the example from page 133 on the board.
- ❑ Explain it to the students.

ANSWER KEY

Answers will vary. Here is an example:

The Rite of Passage: Graduation

Previous Status	Transition	New Status
college student	→ graduation	→ adult who can work and support himself or herself

Steps (Details)

complete coursework

take and pass exams

apply for graduation

rent cap and gown

invite family and friends

go to graduation ceremony

receive diploma

celebrate with family and friends

Symbols are the *cap and gown*, which represent the medieval dress of an academy, and the *diploma*, which represents the degree that the university awards the student.

EXPANSION ACTIVITY

- If students are from different countries, have those from the same country or region work together on a rite of passage.

- If students are from the same country, have them choose different rites of passage and work together in groups on the same one.

- If there is time, have them do research on the Internet and make a poster or PowerPoint presentation about the rite of passage.

- Tell them to share their findings with the class.

New Days, New Ways: Changing Rites of Passage

Before You Read

1 Identifying the Main Idea and Writing a Summary

Best Practice

Making Use of Academic Content

Activities such as this will help expand students' ability to locate main ideas in an academic text. With practice, they will learn to find them and summarize information in a paragraph quickly and accurately.

❑ Read the directions.

❑ Remind students **not** to use a dictionary during this part of the lesson.

❑ Check the answers when students finish.

ANSWER KEY

Answers may vary.

[A] Main Idea: *Anyone can now experience a Native American vision quest, for a fee.*

 Summary: *Although some Native Americans do not approve, several companies and organizations are offering non-Indians the opportunity (for a fee) to experience a vision quest that is similar to the traditional one.*

[B] Main Idea: *Instead of going into debt to get married, Emirati grooms can now have group weddings.*

 Summary: *The government of the United Arab Emirates (UAE) started a marriage fund to help young men stay out of debt when they get married. If they marry women from the UAE, they can have a lavish feast with entertainment.*

[C] Main Idea: *These days, many Japanese couples get married in Western-style Christian weddings.*

 Summary: *Instead of the traditional ceremonies of the past, many Japanese couples dress in Western clothes (tuxedo and long, white dress). They get married in a church using Christian scriptures and hymns, and exchange vows and kiss.*

[D] Main Idea: *Couples in Western countries are also looking for a different wedding experience.*

 Summary: *Besides unusual places, they are considering traditional weddings in other cultures, as in Goa, India, where they can be married in a typical Hindu ceremony.*

[E] Main Idea: *People are also turning to unusual funerals.*

 Summary: *In countries like Malaysia, musical groups sing in different languages and play a variety of music at different kinds of funerals. In other countries, they send their ashes into space, or preserve a dead body doing a favorite activity.*

Strategy

Identifying Opinions

■ Write these words on the board:

 FACT information proven to be true

 OPINION ideas that people may disagree about

■ Read the directions for the first part and tell the class to repeat the words after you.

Examples

bad (-ly)	exquisite	good (well)	surprising
beautiful	favorite	horrible	too
brilliant	fun	interesting	
wonderful (-ly)			

2 Distinguishing Facts from Opinions

- ❏ Read the directions.
- ❏ Tell the students to work as quickly as possible.
- ❏ Check the answers when students finish.

ANSWER KEY

1. fact 2. opinion 3. fact 4. opinion 5. opinion
6. fact 7. fact 8. opinion 9. fact 10. opinion

3 Discussing the Reading: Conducting a Survey

Best Practice

Cultivating Critical Thinking

Activities such as this allow students to engage in critical thinking as they survey other students about a rite of passage in their culture. By conducting a survey, they will arrive at conclusions about their peers' opinions regarding traditional and non-traditional wedding ceremonies.

- ❏ Read the directions.
- ❏ Tell students to fill in the chart.
- ❏ Do the following **Expansion Activity**.

REPRODUCIBLE EXPANSION ACTIVITY

- ■ The aim of this activity is to have students take a survey of their classmates on the topic of weddings.
- ■ Photocopy and distribute **Black Line Master 28** "What Kind of Wedding . . . ?" on page BLM28 of this Teacher's Edition.

- ■ Have students interview their classmates, or let them leave the classroom and interview other students.
- ■ Give them 20–30 minutes to complete the survey.
- ■ If students have access to a computer lab, have them make a bar graph comparing the data (traditional vs. non-traditional and males vs. females).
- ■ When they finish, have them share their findings with the class.

Responding in Writing

SUMMARIZING A WHOLE READING

- ■ Call on different students to read the directions.
- ■ Write these points on the board:

  —Change sentence structure:

active	→	passive
passive	→	active

  —Use synonyms

  —Keep technical terms

4 Practice

- ❏ Have students choose one of the two readings they have read in this chapter to summarize.
- ❏ Have them write a one-paragraph summary alone and then compare it to that of another student.
- ❏ When they have compared their summaries, collect and check them.

5 **Writing Your Own Ideas**

> **Best Practice**
>
> **Activating Prior Knowledge**
>
> Activities such as applying a concept from a reading to their personal experience will help students understand it better. Writing a letter to a family member will enable them to explore a topic and perhaps come to a better understanding of it.

❏ Read the directions.

❏ Have students choose one of the topics listed and write you a letter for homework.

❏ The next day, collect the letters. Pass them around to different students in the class to read.

❏ Tell students to read them and write the main idea of each letter at the bottom.

❏ Then have students write a response to the letter on the back of the paper, telling their opinion on the topic. When students finish, have them give the letters back to the person who wrote them.

❏ After they have read them, collect and check them.

1 Determining Categories

Best Practice

Scaffolding Instruction

Activities such as this will allow students to remember vocabulary better by scaffolding instruction. The words they have just learned from the reading can be categorized into semantic groups and used as a scaffold upon which they can integrate new vocabulary.

❑ Read the directions.

❑ Ask students to do the activity quickly.

❑ Check the answers with the class.

ANSWER KEY

1. praying, chanting, wailing

2. priests, monks

3. coffin, cremation, deceased

4. organization, tribe, community, society

5. hug, wail, shout

6. proposal, wedding, coming-of-age

ANALYZING WORD ROOTS AND PREFIXES

■ Read the directions.

■ Read the **Prefixes** and **Word Roots** and ask students to read the **Meanings**.

---

2 Analyzing Word Roots and Prefixes

❑ Read the directions.

❑ Have students do the activity quickly.

❑ Check the answers.

ANSWER KEY

1. e 2. c 3. a 4. c 5. c 6. e 7. a 8. e

3 Focusing on Words from the Academic Word List

❑ Read the directions.

❑ Have students do the activity quickly.

❑ Check the answers.

ANSWER KEY

1. transition 2. status 3. incorporation
4. previous 5. vision 6. physically 7. community

4 Searching the Internet

Best Practice

Interacting with Others

Activities such as this will encourage students to explore a topic of interest with their peers. They will develop the skills of working together to find information and organizing it in a logical way to present it to the class.

❑ Read the directions.

❑ Have students look at the choices.

❑ Ask them to choose one and find a partner who chose the same one.

❑ Tell them to do the **Expansion Activity** together.

EXPANSION ACTIVITY

■ The purpose of this activity is to encourage students to do research on a topic presented in the readings.

■ Photocopy and distribute **Black Line Master 29** "Rites of Passage Redone" on page BLM29 of this Teacher's Edition.

■ Allow students to choose a topic and search the Internet with others who have chosen the same one.

■ Have them download a photo or prepare an outline on the board to present their topic to the class.

■ Remind students that each one in the group must speak during the presentation.

■ Have the other students write down one or two questions to ask the group after their presentation.

TOPIC-SENTENCE PATTERNS

- Write these sentences from the first three paragraphs on the board:

  [A] Rites of passage are not found only in indigenous cultures. They are universal, occurring in all cultures, and include certain birthdays, coming-of-age rituals, weddings, and funerals.

  [B] Anthropologists use the term *rite of passage* for a ceremony or ritual of transition that marks a person's change from one status or social position to another.

  [C] Many cultures have a rite of passage that marks the birth of a baby. In Korean tradition, the rite begins during the woman's pregnancy.

- Read the directions.

- Call on different students to read the paragraphs.

1 Practice

- ❏ Read the directions

- ❏ Tell students to read the passage quickly. Write a beginning and ending time on the board (10–15 minutes).

- ❏ When time is up, tell them to stop reading.

- ❏ Put the students in pairs.

- ❏ Read the directions for the activity after the reading and have the students write down their answers.

- ❏ Check the answers when they finish.

ANSWER KEY
Answers may vary.

1. [A] Every society has rites of passage that fit its culture.
2. [B] Learning to drive in the United States reflects values of American culture and can be compared to other rites of passage in other cultures.
3. [C] The timing of learning to drive has great significance for the majority of Americans.
4. [D] Both family and school prepare teenagers for the transition toward adulthood, specifically learning how to drive.
5. [E] American society treasures state-issued permits and reveres the processes for obtaining them.
6. [F] America's cultural preoccupation with money is also addressed in the ritual of getting a driver's license.
7. [G] Being a driver brings deep-seated American values into play.
8. [H] Driving represents a passage from childhood into adulthood.

Self-Assessment Log

- ❏ Read the directions aloud and have students check vocabulary they learned in the chapter and are prepared to use.

- ❏ Have students check the strategies practiced in the chapter (or the degree to which they learned them). They have actually used all these strategies in Chapter 10.

- ❏ Put students in small groups. Ask students to find the information or an activity related to each strategy in the group.

- ❏ Tell students to find definitions in the chapter for any words they did not check.

EXPANSION ACTIVITY

- The aim of this activity is to have students practice the parts of speech of words in the **Target Vocabulary** and **Vocabulary List** in **PART 1**.

- Photocopy and distribute **Black Line Master 30** "Parts of Speech" on page BLM30 of this Teacher's Edition.

- Read the directions.

- Tell students to work individually and then in pairs.

- Have students check their work using a dictionary.

BLM 1

Name _____ Date _____

Can You Tell Me About Your Schooling?

Directions: Take this paper and a pencil and interview a classmate. Ask your classmate the questions below. When you finish, introduce your partner to the class.

1. Where did you go to school—city, town or country? Public or private?

School	Area	Public/Private
a) elementary school		
b) middle school		
c) high school		

2. Were the schools mixed or only for boys or girls?

3. Did you have to wear a uniform? If so, what did it look like? If not, what kind of clothing did you wear to school?

4. How did you get to and from school every day?

5. What kind of teachers did you have? (strict / kind / boring / interesting / old / young / etc.)?

6. Who was your favorite teacher? Why?

7. What subjects were you good in / not so good in?

8. What other activities did you participate in at school, such as sports or clubs?

Name _____   Date _____

Can You Tell Me Your Opinion?

Directions: Take this paper and a pencil and interview five people. Ask them their opinion about the positive and negative aspects of the educational system in their country. Take notes on their answers. When you finish, report your findings to the class.

Name/Country	Positive Aspects of Educational System	Negative Aspects of Educational System
1. Name: Country:		
2. Name: Country:		
3. Name: Country:		
4. Name: Country:		
5. Name: Country:		

Name _____   Date _____

Find A College Or University That . . .

Directions: Take this paper and a pencil and go to the computer lab with a partner. Take turns looking up the following information. When you finish, share your notes with another pair of students. Then give this paper to your teacher.

Find a college or university that . . .

❑ is near a river: _Boston University_   _Boston, MA (USA)_   _www.bu.edu_ _____

❑ has a virtual (online) tour: _____

❑ offers classes in horseback riding: _____

❑ allows students to spend one year studying abroad: _____

❑ offers classes in many African languages (such as Amharic, Yoruba, Swahili, and Zulu): _____

❑ has an art museum: _____

❑ _____ (your choice): _____

Share your answers with another pair of students and copy their answers here:

_____

_____

_____

_____

_____

_____

_____

_____

_____

_____

_____

_____

_____

_____

_____

BLM 4

Name _____   Date _____

Major Cities

Directions: Choose a country. Draw a simple map of that country. Write the names of three major cities.

Country _____

Cities _____

Look up your country online and write the following information below about **one** of the cities. Present your findings to the class.

1. Population: _____

2. Problems in the city: _____

3. Mass transit system: _____

4. Recycling program: _____

5. Homeless people/programs: _____

6. Environmental programs: _____

Name _____ Date _____

City Life In The Future

Directions: Take this paper and a pencil and interview three people. Ask them their opinion about city life in the future. Take notes on their answers. When you finish, report your findings to the class.

1. Name	
Will city life be better or worse than it is today?	**Why?** **1.** **2.**
How will city life be different from what it is today?	**Predictions:**
2. Name	
Will city life be better or worse than it is today?	**Why?** **1.** **2.**
How will city life be different from what it is today?	**Predictions:**
3. Name	
Will city life be better or worse than it is today?	**Why?** **1.** **2.**
How will city life be different from what it is today?	**Predictions:**

BLM 6

Name _____   Date _____

English-Language Newspapers

Directions: Take this paper and a pencil and go to the computer lab or use your own computer. With a partner, use a search engine (like Google) to find the name of an English-language newspaper in the country assigned by your instructor. You can go to *www.newspapersonline.com*. Read an article about the capital city of that country and write about the main ideas and details. When you finish, report your findings to the class.

Country: _____

Name of newspaper: _____

Main Ideas	Details
1.	1.
	2.
	3.
2.	1.
	2.
	3.
3.	1.
	2.
	3.
4.	1.
	2.
	3.

Name _____ Date _____

Venn Diagrams

Directions: Take this paper and a pencil and choose 2 sets of persons, places, or things that have both similarities <u>and</u> differences. When you finish, share your diagrams with two other students.

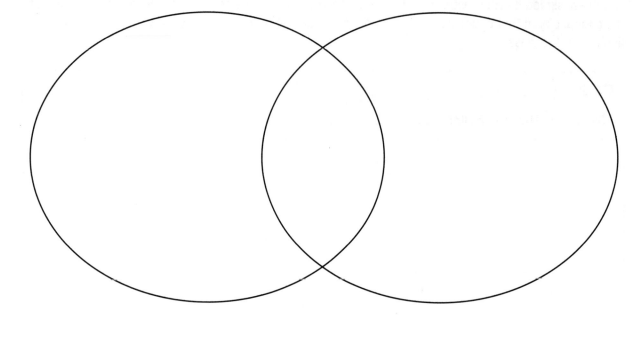

_____

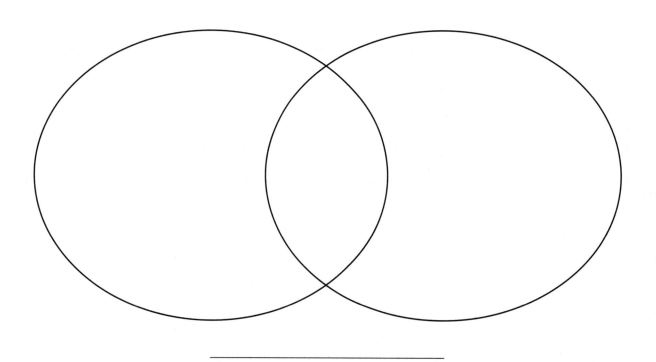

_____

BLM 8

Name _____   Date _____

Consumer Organizations In My Country

Directions: Take this paper and with a partner look up a consumer organization in your country. Make sure it is different from those of the other students. When you finish, report your findings to the class.

Name and Logo		
History (When? Who?)		
Purpose		
Programs or Events		
Sources of Funding		
Number of Members		

Name _____ Date _____

Analyzing Advertisements

A. Choose a product with your group. Each member will look in a different magazine for an advertisement of this product and bring it to class. Write short answers to these questions about your advertisement. Share your answers with your group.

1. What is your group's product? _____

2. How does your advertisement show the product? _____

3. Are there any people in the picture? How do they look? What are they doing? _____

4. What do you think this product does for them? _____

5. How do you think they feel about this product? _____

6. What are some of the words or expressions used in the advertisement? _____

_____

7. What do they mean? _____

8. How do you feel about this product? _____

9. Would you buy it? Why or why not? _____

10. What kind of psychology is used? _____

B. Write a short paragraph about your advertisement. Include some of the answers to the questions above. Then show your advertisement to the class and analyze it.

In this advertisement, we see . . .

_____

_____

_____

_____

_____

_____

_____

_____

BLM 10

Name _____ Date _____

Cell Phone Use

Directions: Every time you use your cell phone, put a check (✓) in one of the columns. Later you will use these data to make a pie chart to show the percentage of use for each category.

Day	Made call	Received call	Sent text	Received text	Sent image	Received image
Monday						
Tuesday						
Wednesday						
Thursday						
Friday						
Saturday						
Sunday						
Total						

❑ Put a check each time you make or receive a call, send or receive text messages or images (photos or videos).

❑ Show your cell phone log to your partner every day.

❑ At the end of the week, write the total in each column.

❑ Take your log to the computer lab with your partner and make pie charts of your cell phone use. If you are not sure how to do this, ask for help.

❑ Share your pie charts with the class.

❑ Give your log to the teacher. A classmate will make pie charts of the cell phone use of men and of women and the whole class.

❑ Put all the pie charts on a poster board or bulletin board to share with the class.

BLM 11

Name _____ Date _____

Survey of Globalized Countries

Directions: Take this paper and a pencil and interview 10 people in the category your group has chosen (nationality or age group). When you finish, make a bar graph and share your data displays with other groups in the class.

Questions:

1. Do you have a cell phone?
2. Do you have a computer?
3. Are you interested in the politics of your country?
4. Does your country have many international visitors?
5. Does your country have a strong economy?

Nationality or Age Group	Cell Phone Y/N	Computer Y/N	Politics Y/N	International Visitors Y/N	Strong Economy Y/N
1 M					
2 M					
3 M					
4 M					
5 M					
6 F					
7 F					
8 F					
9 F					
10 F					
Total					

Answers: Yes = Y; No = N

M=Male; F=Female

BLM 12

Name _____ Date _____

Online Job Boards

A. Underline the website that you and your partner chose in class (www.careerbuilder.com; hotjobs.yahoo.com; jobsjobsjobs.com; www.jobster.com; www.jobweb.com; www.monster.com) and find it on the Internet. Explore the online job board and answer the following questions.

Useful job-related information:

1. _____

2. _____

3. _____

4. _____

5. _____

B. Rate this online job site by circling a number for each category.

	worst ———— satisfactory ———— best				
Attractive site	1	2	3	4	5
Easy to find information	1	2	3	4	5
Many jobs listed	1	2	3	4	5
Process clear	1	2	3	4	5
Easy to ask questions	1	2	3	4	5

C. If you have a résumé or curriculum vitae, apply online for one of the jobs that you are qualified for. Report to the class on the response that you get.

Name _____   Date _____

Fads in Your Country

Directions: Take this paper and a pencil and interview 5 other students. Ask them about different fads in their country. When you finish, share your findings with the class.

Name	Country	Clothing	Food	Music	Activities
1.					
2.					
3.					
4.					
5.					

Compare your answers to see if there are any similarities in fads among different countries.

_____

_____

_____

_____

_____

_____

Name _____   Date _____

Extreme Sports

Directions: Take this paper and a pencil and go to the computer lab with a partner. Look on a website about extreme sports; a few are listed below. Find two extreme sports that you and your partner would like to try. When you finish, report your findings to the class.

http://www.extreme.com/

http://expn.go.com/expn/index

http://www.allextremesports.com/

http://www.guinnessworldrecords.com/

http://www.extremesportscafe.com/main.html

	Extreme Sport 1. _____	**Extreme Sport** 2. _____
Equipment needed		
Practice area		
Skills needed		
Reasons to try it		

Name _____ Date _____

Reality TV Shows

Directions: Take this paper and a pencil and go to the computer lab with a partner or do the assignment at home. Look up a reality show on the Internet in the country you have chosen. Write the answers to the questions. When you finish, give a short report to the class.

1. Name of Reality TV Show: _____

2. Country: _____

3. Summary: _____

_____

_____

_____

_____

_____

_____

_____

4. Participants/Winner: _____

5. Opinion of the show: _____

_____

_____

6. Ask another student if they would like to watch this show? Ask them Why or Why Not?

_____

_____

_____

Name _____ Date _____

Analyzing a Country

Directions: With a partner, choose a country and look at one of these websites. Locate the information below. When you finish, share your findings with the class.

http://www.nationsonline.org/
http://www.infoplease.com/countries.html
http://www.cia.gov/cia/publications/factbook/

1. Name of Country / Region of the World: _____

   _____

2. Geography / Border Countries: _____

   _____

3. Capital / Major Cities: _____

   _____

4. Climate / Agricultural Products: _____

   _____

5. Natural Resources / Industries: _____

   _____

6. Imports / Exports: _____

   _____

7. Transportation: _____

   _____

8. Communications: _____

   _____

9. Unemployment Rate: _____

   _____

10. GDP* / GNI (PPP)**: _____

* GDP = Gross Domestic Product, i.e., the value of everything produced in this country
** GNI (PPP) = Gross National Income (Purchasing Power Parity), i.e., what one person earns in this country compared to what this money can buy in other countries

BLM 17

Name _____ Date _____

A Different Kind of Vacation

Directions: Take this paper and a pencil and go to the computer lab with a partner. Look on a website about international study, travel, or volunteering, and fill in the chart below. When you have finished, present your findings to the class.

Country Region			
Activities Available			
Activity Chosen			
Reasons for Going			
Trip & Airfare		**Dates of Travel**	
Daily Schedule			
People to Meet			
Things to Do			
Things to Learn			

Name _____   Date _____

Matching Idioms

Directions: Take this paper and a pencil and copy the idioms from the board after the class activity.

1. stop the progress of movement   _____

2. alone; not with a group   _____

3. looking for; hoping to find   _____

4. travels, goes   _____

5. on a train   _____

6. detective   _____

7. look for and find   _____

8. mystery   _____

9. arrived in   _____

10. travel in a simple way   _____

11. go from place to place   _____

12. actively participate in something   _____

13. travel slowly   _____

Name _____   Date _____

Find Someone Who . . .

Directions: Take this paper and a pencil. Stand up, move around the classroom. Ask classmates the questions below. When someone answers *yes*, write his or her name on the line. When someone answers *no*, ask another question. When you finish, introduce your partner to the class.

Example: A: Do you have a dog?

B. No, I have a bird, a canary.

A: How does it communicate with you?

B: It sings to me.

A: Great. What's your name?

Do you have . . .?	How does it/do they communicate with you?
1. a dog? Name: _____	
2. a cat? Name: _____	
3. a bird? Name: _____	
4. a fish or turtle? Name: _____	
5. a mouse, rat, hamster or gerbil? Name: _____	
6. a horse, donkey or camel? Name: _____	
7. more than one pet? Name: _____	
8. animals outside your house? Name: _____	
9. animals that you ride? Name: _____	

Name _____   Date _____

Toys for Girls and Boys

Directions: Take this paper and a pencil and look at two different websites with your group. In the first column, make a list of three toys advertised for girls, three for boys, and three for both. In the second column, put *SI* for *social-interactive* and *TO* for *task-oriented*. In the third column, write a short description of how children might play with the toys. Be prepared to present your list to the class.

Toys for Girls	SI/TO	Description of Game/Activity
1. *My Little Pony*	*SI*	*Each girl takes a pony to one girl's house to have a "pony party." Each girl "talks" for her pony as it plays with the other ponies. Game ends when party ends.*
2.		
3.		
Toys for Boys	**SI/TO**	**Description of Game/Activity**
1. *Action figures*	*TO*	*Each boy takes an action figure outside to play with. They all fight together against a common enemy. Game ends when enemy is overcome.*
2.		
3.		
Toys for Both	**SI/TO**	**Description of Game/Activity**
1.		
2.		
3.		

Name _____ Date _____

Slang Expressions

Directions: Take this paper and a pencil and look at the slang expressions in Part I. Try to guess the meaning of each one and write it in Standard American English (SAE). Your instructor will help you. Then think of words or phrases in your language that come from English in Part II. Write them the way they are spelled in your language and in English. Then write a "pure" word in your language with the same/similar meaning. Be prepared to present your list to the class.

Part I

Slang expressions	Standard American English
'S up?	
A'ight.	
Latah!	
Gotcha!	
W'sat?	
Dunno.	

Part II

Your Language	English	"Pure" Word

BLM 22

Name _____   Date _____

Traveling the Silk Road

Directions: With a partner, choose a country or region along the Silk Road and one of the products grown or made there that was transported by the merchants in caravans. Use the Internet to locate information on your topic. When you finish, share your findings with the class.

1. Name of country or region: _____

   _____

2. History of settlers or migrants: _____

   _____

3. Major cities: _____

   _____

4. Climate and agriculture: _____

   _____

5. Natural resources and products: _____

   _____

6. How product was made: _____

   _____

7. Which countries bought and used the product: _____

   _____

8. Present-day use of product: _____

   _____

Name _____   Date _____

Beauty Treatments

Directions: Take this paper and a pencil and go to the computer lab with a partner or small group. Look on a website about beauty treatments and fill in the chart below. When you have finished, present your findings to the class.

Name of treatment	
Place of treatment	
People giving it/ training	
People getting it	
Equipment needed	
Steps in treatment	
Cost per visit	
Results of treatment	
Benefits/ Dangers	

BLM 24

Name _____   Date _____

Spelling and Synonyms

Directions: Take this paper and a pencil and write the words that your teacher or classmates dictate to you in the first column. Then write a synonym or meaning for the word in the second column.

Spelling	Synonym/Meaning
1.	
2.	
3.	
4.	
5.	
6.	
7.	
8.	
9.	
10.	
11.	
12.	
13.	
14.	
15.	

Name _____ Date _____

Improving Your Brain

Directions: With a partner, choose one of the suggestions given in paragraph [H] and [I], or others that you can think of. Use the Internet to locate information on your topic. When you finish, share your findings with the class.

Good for your brain	Bad for your brain
Activities:	**Activities:**
Food/Drink:	**Food/Drink:**
Other:	**Other:**
What I'll start doing:	**What I'll stop doing:**

Name _____ Date _____

Violence and Genetics

Directions: Take this paper and a pencil and go to the computer lab with a partner or small group. Look for an article on the Internet about the link between violence and genetics and fill in the chart below. When you have finished, present your findings to the class.

Name of article and author(s)	
Place where study was done	
Group of people studied	
Background of people	
Scientific explanation	
Other comments	
Possible treatments	
Social consequences	
Prevention of violence	
Your opinion	

Name _____   Date _____

Parts of Speech

Directions: Take this paper and a pencil and write the parts of speech in each column without using a dictionary. Some words do not have all four word forms. When you finish, check your answers with a partner, using a dictionary if necessary.

NOUN	VERB	ADJECTIVE	ADVERB
1. evidence	———	———	
2.	imply	———	———
3.	———	insightful	
4.	———		intelligently
5. maturity			
6.	memorize	———	———
7.		personal	
8.	———		psychologically
9. logic	———		
10.	involve		———
11. ———	———	mental	
12.	———		traditionally

Name _____   Date _____

What Kind of Wedding . . . ?

Directions: Take this paper and a pencil and interview the students in your class or outside your class. Record how many people answer "traditional" and "nontraditional." Take notes on the reasons for their answers.

What kind of wedding do you prefer: traditional or nontraditional?	
Traditional	**Nontraditional**
Why? What are your favorite parts?	What is your idea of a good nontraditional wedding? (What are the elements?)
_____	_____
_____	_____
_____	_____
_____	_____
_____	_____
_____	_____
_____	_____
_____	_____
_____	_____
_____	_____
_____	_____
_____	_____
_____	_____
# of males	# of males
# of females	# of females

Name _____ Date _____

Rites of Passage Redone

Directions: Take this paper and a pencil and go to the computer lab with a partner or small group. Look for an article on the Internet about nontraditional rites of passage and fill in the chart below. When you have finished, present your findings to the class.

Rite of passage	
People who did it	
Place where it was done	
Way it was done	
People who attended	
How much it cost	
Other comments	
Would you like to do it?	
How would you change it?	
Other comments	

Name _____ Date _____

Parts of Speech

Directions: Take this paper and a pencil and write the parts of speech in each column without using a dictionary. Some words do not have all four word forms. When you finish, check your answers with a partner, using a dictionary if necessary.

NOUN	VERB	ADJECTIVE	ADVERB
1.	chant		———
2. community	———		
3.	cremate		———
4. incorporation			———
5. ———	———	indigenous	
6. negotiations			———
7.	———	physical	
8. ———	———		previously
9. rite	———		
10.			transitionally
11.	vary	———	———
12. wail			———

BLM #18 Answer Key

1. hold (someone) back 2. on (one's) own 3. in the market for 4. runs 5. on board 6. private eye 7. track down 8. whodunit 9. pulled into 10. rough it 11. get around 12. hands-on experience 13. take (one's) time

BLM #21 Answer Key

1. What's up? 2. All right 3. See you later! 4. I got you! = I understand! 5. What's that? 6. I don't know.

BLM #24 Answer Key

Answers may vary.

BLM #27 Answer Key

1. evidently 2. implication 3. insight; insightfully
4. intelligence; intelligent 5. mature; mature; maturely
6. memory/memorization 7. person; personify; personally 8. psychology/psychologist; psychological
9. logical; logically 10. involvement; involved
11. mentally 12. tradition; traditional

BLM #30 Answer Key

1. chant; chanting 2. communal; communally
3. cremation; cremated 4. incorporate; incorporated
5. indigenously 6. negotiate; negotiable/negotiated
7. physician/physique; physically 8. previous
9. ritual; ritually 10. transition; transition/transit; transitional 11. variety/variation 12. wail; wailing

Chapter 1 Test

Homeschooling

Section I Reading Comprehension Answer these questions about the reading passage.
(3 points each)

A   One of the trends in education in the United States in recent times has been homeschooling —teaching children at home instead of at school. About 1.5 million children, or 2.5% of the school-age population, are presently taught at home. There are several reasons for this movement: lack of good schools in some neighborhoods, the desire to include religion in coursework, and parental disagreement with classroom practices in public schools.

B   As you read in Chapter 1, poorer areas of the United States generally have poorer schools. Teachers may not be well trained, and equipment may not be as modern as in richer schools. Some parents think that teaching their children at home is better than sending them to an inferior school.

C   Other parents, often Christians, want their children to learn about God in school. While there *are* private schools that teach classes in religion, they tend to be expensive. Parents can save money by buying materials from Christian education companies and teaching their children at home.

D   Another group of parents disagree with the way schools are run or the way children are taught. They want a less rigid atmosphere in which their children can choose the subjects they want to learn or study in nontraditional ways. They can provide their children with more flexibility if they homeschool them.

E   People often wonder if homeschooled children learn as much as those in traditional schools. Organizations like the National Home Education Research Institute say that they do. Many educational companies put together courses that contain books, DVDs, and online (Internet) lessons and tests. Students who complete these courses are just as capable of entering top universities and graduating with honors as those who attend traditional schools. They are also able to get good jobs and perform well in the workplace.

F   Although some educators, critics of homeschooling, may not want to accept this fact, many children taught at home actually do better than many taught at school. They are more interested in studying and more comfortable with their own learning style. Instead of being motivated to compete for the highest grade, they are motivated by love of learning.
(353 words)

1. The number of children who are taught at home is _____.
- (A) 1.5 million
- (B) 1.5% of the school-age population
- (C) 2.5% higher than last year
- (D) 2.5 million

2. Parents who want their children to have a religious education _____.

 (A) always send them to expensive schools

 (B) sometimes buy materials and teach their children at home

 (C) do not want their children to learn about God

 (D) never send money to Christian education companies

3. Some parents homeschool their children because _____.

 (A) there are good schools in their neighborhood

 (B) they disagree with public school practices

 (C) they do not want their children to study religion

 (D) they have enough money for a private school

4. Critics of homeschooling think that children _____.

 (A) are more comfortable with their own learning style

 (B) are more interested in studying at home

 (C) compete at home for the highest grade

 (D) in traditional schools do better that children schooled at home

5. Generally, children who are homeschooled _____.

 (A) are able to enter good universities

 (B) are not successful at work

 (C) cannot get very good jobs

 (D) do not do well in traditional schools

Section II Strategy Look back at the highlighted words and then do the activity below.
(3 points each)

1. Homeschooling means _____.

 (A) bringing teachers from school to home

 (B) buying materials at school and using them at home

 (C) driving children from home to school

 (D) teaching children at home instead of at school

2. Some courses have online lessons that can be found _____.

 (A) in schools

 (B) on the Internet

 (C) on the same day

 (D) one after the other

3. Some of the critics of homeschooling are _____.

 (A) bus drivers

 (B) parents

 (C) educators

 (D) researchers

4. The word inferior in paragraph B probably means _____.

 (A) modern

 (B) poorer

 (C) richer

 (D) well-trained

5. The word rigid in paragraph D is closest in meaning to _____.

- (A) boring
- (B) competitive
- (C) difficult
- (D) inflexible

Section III New Words Fill in the blanks with words from the Academic Word List from Chapter 1. **(4 points each)**

assignments	contrasts	creative	culture	goal
involves	lecture	methods	primary	traditions

When children are homeschooled, the mother usually teaches them. Because they are at home

all day, she has to think of _____ ways to keep their attention. For example, if
                                    1

a science lesson for _____ school children is about how seeds grow, she plants
                              2

seeds with them. If a lesson _____ the weather, she will ask them to observe
                                        3

and record the weather. She doesn't _____ the children, but rather, gives them
                                                4

interesting _____ to do. Her teaching _____ include both
                    5   6

active and passive learning, like watching real plants grow and then reading about them. Or

she might teach them about another _____ by visiting a museum, eating food
                                              7

from another country, or watching a foreign film with them. They can learn about other people's

_____ through these activities. Because of _____ in the
          8   9

lessons, the children don't get bored. Her _____ is to make homeschooling both
                                                        10

interesting and fun so that her children will learn as much as students in traditional schools.

Section IV Building Vocabulary Find the words in the box that complete the following phrases and write them in the blanks. Some words can be used more than one time. **(3 points each)**

at	attend	in	on
other	take	to	of

1. Some children do not _____ school; their parents teach them at home.

2. Some people think that these children are _____ a disadvantage.

3. Others think that they have everything available _____ children in traditional schools.

4. _____ the one hand, they may be studying alone. On the _____ hand, their classes are flexible.

5. Because _____ technology, homeschooled children can get lessons from the Internet.

6. They also have access _____ online activities and chat-rooms with other homeschoolers.

7. Just like other children, they must _____ exams at the end of each year.

8. When homeschooled children go to live _____ a dormitory _____ a college campus, many are going to school for the first time!

TOTAL _____ /100 pts.

Chapter 2 Test

Asthma

Section I Reading Comprehension Answer these questions about the reading passage.
(3 points each)

A   Respiratory illnesses such as asthma have increased greatly in the past few decades. It
is estimated that 5% of the population in the United States has asthma, which is a chronic
disease, that is, it affects a person over a long period of time. It may begin before a child is
10 years old, or it may begin in adulthood. Childhood asthma usually disappears around the
age of 20, but adults who get it later may have it all their lives.

B   People who suffer from asthma have difficulty breathing because the airways in their lungs
contract when a trigger causes a reaction. Among the triggers of asthma are indoor and
outdoor pollutants, according to doctors. Since pollution has become more common, the
number of people affected by this disorder has risen. Indoor pollutants include cigarette
smoke, dirt, insects, and even pets like dogs or cats. Outdoor pollutants include chemicals,
dust, and smog, that is, smoke from factories or transport vehicles like buses and trucks.

C   People with asthma usually carry an inhaler in case of an attack. This inhaler contains
medicine that they breathe in, making the contracted airways in the lungs expand so that
they can breathe normally again. For a few people with severe asthma, medicine can also be
given by injection -- in other words, it can be applied under the skin with a needle every few
weeks to prevent attacks.

D   While it is not possible to cure this condition, people who suffer from it are advised to
avoid pollutants. Parents with asthmatic children are told not to smoke in the house and
not to keep long-haired pets . They need to clean the house frequently and keep it free of
insects. Asthmatic adults are told to avoid outdoor areas with a lot of pollution and working
environments with a lot of chemicals.

E   Scientists continue to search for a cure for asthma, but instead of waiting for one, people
with asthma can take an active role in protecting themselves. By avoiding asthma triggers,
carrying an inhaler, living in a clean, smoke-free house, and working in a pollutant-free
place, they can live healthier lives. (352 words)

1. Childhood asthma usually _____.
- (A) appears when children are 5
- (B) appears before children are 10
- (C) disappears after children are 10
- (D) disappears before children are 20

2. Asthma attacks may be triggered by _____.
- Ⓐ chemicals and smog
- Ⓑ dogs and cats
- Ⓒ dust and insects
- Ⓓ all of the above

3. To control asthma, most people _____.
- Ⓐ carry inhalers
- Ⓑ get injections
- Ⓒ go to the hospital
- Ⓓ stay home

4. To avoid having asthma attacks, people can _____.
- Ⓐ keep fish or turtles as pets
- Ⓑ ride more trucks and buses
- Ⓒ start smoking
- Ⓓ stop cleaning their house

5. Asthmatics should _____.
- Ⓐ carry several inhalers
- Ⓑ get injections every week
- Ⓒ protect themselves from pollutants
- Ⓓ wait for scientists to find a cure

Section II Strategy Look at the highlighted words and then match Column A with Column B.
(3 points each)

Column A	Column B
1. asthmatic	**a.** asthma
2. chronic	**b.** buses and trucks
3. indoor pollutants	**c.** cats and dogs
4. inhaler	**d.** causes a reaction
5. injection	**e.** chemicals, dust, and smog
6. long-haired pets	**f.** cigarette smoke, dirt, insects
7. outdoor pollutants	**g.** contains medicine for asthmatics
8. respiratory illness	**h.** having difficulty breathing
9. triggers	**i.** medicine given under skin with needle
10. vehicles	**j.** over a long period of time

Section III New Words Fill in the blanks with words from the Academic Word List from the Chapter 2. **(3 points each)**

access	environment	established	focused	global
method	predict	residents	solve	transportation

Asthma is usually common in countries where there is a lot of pollution in the

_____ from industry and different types of _____ such as
1   2

ships and trains. However, it has become a _____ problem; that is, countries
3

with large rural areas also have high rates of asthma. A doctor in Jamaica decided to find out

why asthma was increasing among young rural _____ where pollution didn't
4

seem to be a problem. She noticed that more children had asthma attacks when it was windy.

She asked a scientist who was studying weather patterns to find out if there was a connection.

The scientist, also a woman, developed a _____ of collecting what was blowing
5

in the wind. Together they _____ a connection between the amount of dust
6

in the wind and the number of asthmas attacks on the island. The scientist also discovered that

some of the dust had actually blown to Jamaica from the dry regions of Africa across the Atlantic

Ocean. With a way to _____ when asthma attacks were going to occur, the
7

doctor _____ on giving the rural population _____ to weather
8   9

forecasts so that asthmatics would stay indoors on windy days. A public health campaign helped

to _____ the problem and lower the number of asthma attacks.
10

Section IV Building Vocabulary Write the missing noun, verb, adjective or adverb in the numbered boxes. **(2 points each)**

Noun	Verb	Adjective	Adverb
difference	(1)	different	(2)
(3)	pollute	(4)	————
prediction	(5)	predictable	(6)
(7)	save	(8)	safely
(9)	solve	(10)	————

Complete the sentences below with words from the preceding chart. Use one word from each line of the chart. **(1 point each)**

11. Countries around the world have _____ rates of asthma, depending on the amount

of pollution.

12. Asthma attacks in Jamaica are _____ because they usually occur when it's windy.

13. The _____ to the problem was to warn asthmatics to stay indoors on windy days.

14. When factories _____ a lake or river, the fish often die.

15. This means that people cannot _____ swim in water that is polluted.

TOTAL ____ /100 pts.

Chapter 3 Test

The Consumers Union

Section I Reading Comprehension Answer these questions about the reading passage.
(3 points each)

A The Consumers Union (CU) was founded in 1936 to give information and advice to the public about goods and services. By doing research in laboratories and conducting tests on products, scientists were able to rate them, or tell if they were good or bad. They started by testing food like milk and cereal—and then personal products like soap and stockings. There were three categories in their ratings: *Best Buy*, *Also Acceptable*, and *Not Acceptable*. Later, CU began testing cars and home appliances, such as fans, radios, and other small machines.

B In the same year it was founded, the organization began publishing a magazine for its members, *Consumers Union Reports*, listing the ratings of products that they tested. In 1940, CU sent out a questionnaire, that is, a list of questions, to its members, asking them to rate the products that they used. This questionnaire became so popular that it has continued until today. In 1942, the magazine's name was changed to *Consumer Reports* and sold to the general public.

C By the 1950s, the number of people buying *Consumer Reports (CR)* reached 400,000. During this decade, the magazine reported on the dangers of tobacco, the poor quality of color TV sets, the contamination of milk by nuclear testing, and other news that was controversial, or caused debate. In the 1960s, the magazine reported that the price of auto insurance varied widely, or was different, among companies. In the 1970s, it reported on the pollution of America's drinking water by factories. These articles won national prizes because they informed the public about problems that needed to be solved.

D In the 1980s, *CR* began publishing special newsletters for different readers on cars, travel, health, and even one for children on how to earn and save money. In the 1990s, the Consumers Union moved to a new testing and research center with 50 modern laboratories in Yonkers, New York. By this time, *CR* had over 5 million magazine readers and 1 million online readers. After 70 years, this organization is still protecting consumers from the false claims of advertisers and the dangers of unsafe products. (352 words)

1. The Consumers Union started to publish a magazine _____.
- (A) in 1936
- (B) in 1940
- (C) in the 1980s
- (D) in the 1990s

2. The magazine was sold only to members until _____.
- (A) 1936
- (B) 1940
- (C) 1942
- (D) 1960

3. In the 1950s, *CR* didn't report on _____.

- Ⓐ bad TV sets
- Ⓑ contaminated milk
- Ⓒ tobacco's dangers
- Ⓓ polluted drinking water

4. The magazine won prizes because _____.

- Ⓐ it rated products
- Ⓑ it told the public about problems
- Ⓒ some products were not acceptable
- Ⓓ there were so many problems

5. After 70 years, people _____.

- Ⓐ are still reading *CR*
- Ⓑ are tired of reading *CR*
- Ⓒ believe the false claims of advertisers
- Ⓓ buy unsafe products

Section II Strategy Look back at the highlighted words and then do the activity below.
(3 points each)

1. To rate means _____.

- Ⓐ to conduct tests on products
- Ⓑ to do research in laboratories
- Ⓒ to tell if products are good or bad
- Ⓓ to test food and personal products

2. Home appliances are _____.

- Ⓐ cars
- Ⓑ milk and cereal
- Ⓒ small machines
- Ⓓ soap and stockings

3. A questionnaire is _____.

- Ⓐ a list of questions
- Ⓑ a magazine
- Ⓒ ratings of products
- Ⓓ so popular.

4. The word controversial in paragraph B probably means _____.

- Ⓐ causing debate
- Ⓑ contamination
- Ⓒ dangerous
- Ⓓ other news

5. The word varied in paragraph C is closest in meaning to _____.

- Ⓐ very cheap
- Ⓑ very expensive
- Ⓒ was changing
- Ⓓ was different

Section III New Words Fill in the blanks with words from the Academic Word List from the Chapter 3. **(3 points each)**

capacity	common knowledge	consumes	economy	funds
grants	influenced	item	sport utility vehicle	success

After reading about the Consumers Union (CU), you may wonder how scientists test

the products. It is _____ that CU buys all the products that it tests. If a
                              1

company sends an _____ , CU returns it because it does not want to be
                             2

_____ by the company. The _____ of its testing is based
          3   4

on the independence of its testing. CU is supported by _____ collected from
                                                                       5

members and _____ from other sources. It does not accept any money from
                         6

companies. To rate a car like a _____ , a driver takes it to the auto-test facility
                                             7

in Connecticut. There he will find out the _____ of the car, or how many people
                                                          8

and how much equipment will fit inside. Next, he will drive it around for several hours to see

what its fuel _____ is, or how much gas it _____ . Then, he
                       9   10

will drive it in rainy and snowy weather and in rocky and hilly areas to see how fast it goes and

how safely it stops. Finally, he and a team of other drivers will look at the data and give the SUV

a rating.

Section IV Building Vocabulary Are the following words nouns or adjectives? On the lines write *n.* for *noun* or *adj.* for *adjective*. (**2 points each**)

_____ **1.** information   _____ **6.** dissatisfaction

_____ **2.** identical   _____ **7.** marketers

_____ **3.** social   _____ **8.** violent

_____ **4.** subsidiary   _____ **9.** influential

_____ **5.** offensive   _____ **10.** advantage

Complete the sentences below with words from the preceding exercise. Use a different word for each sentence. (**2 points each**)

11. _____ try to influence consumers to buy products.

12. Some advertisements are _____ because they are not true.

13. People often show their _____ with a product by returning it.

14. Before you buy a product, get as much _____ about it as possible.

15. You will have an _____ if you compare products before you buy them.

16. If you buy two _____ products, one may not work as well as the other.

17. In a _____ snowstorm, it is dangerous to drive, even in an SUV.

18. A company may have a _____ in another country.

19. If CU allows companies to send them free products, this may be _____ on how CU rates the product.

20. CU performs a _____ service when it tells the public about unsafe products.

TOTAL _____ **/100 pts.**

Chapter 4 Test
Career Change

Section I Reading Comprehension Answer these questions about the reading passage.
(3 points each)

A   People who are thinking about changing careers are often afraid of what will happen if they quit their job. Will they find another one? Will they like another field as well as the one they are in now? Will they be able to grow and advance in a new organization?

B   As these questions come to mind, they should try to figure out the answers so they can reach a decision. Although there is a high rate of unemployment in some countries, there are usually jobs for skilled workers who can use computers or other equipment. Those who have specialized training in these areas can generally find a position without too much effort.

C   The question of whether they'll like another field more than their current one is also a crucial one. While it's nice to dream about having another job, the reality may be that they aren't suited for it. For example, if an architect likes to cook but has no idea about how to run a business, it may be risky for him to open a restaurant. He can cook for his friends on weekends and satisfy his dreams of being a chef in that way.

D   Another good way for a person to find out if she will be successful in a new field is to try it out as a part-time job. Being an event planner sounds glamorous, but helping friends with parties or weddings might show her that it's also very stressful. However, if she has the creativity and organization necessary for such a position, she can continue to plan events for friends until she builds up a reputation. Then she can leave her current job to look for a job in event planning knowing that she'll be successful in this area.

E   Once a person has found his or her specialty and decides on the change, it's necessary to stick with it until the business gets off the ground. This usually takes about five years. If the move has been from one company to another, the person should stay until it is clear he is doing a good job and can advance to a higher position. Following this advice will make the transition smoother and the career change successful. (371 words)

1. According to the reading, people who think about changing careers generally _____.
- Ⓐ quit their jobs
- Ⓑ are afraid of quitting their jobs
- Ⓒ find another one right away
- Ⓓ grow and advance in a new organization

2. There is a high rate of unemployment in some countries, but skilled workers _____.
- Ⓐ lose their jobs
- Ⓑ try to reach a decision
- Ⓒ use computers
- Ⓓ with training can still get jobs

3. If a person dreams about doing another job, _____.
- Ⓐ he is suited for it
- Ⓑ he can run a business
- Ⓒ he still may not be able to do it
- Ⓓ he will be satisfied as a chef

4. Having a part-time job _____.
- Ⓐ is a good way to try another career
- Ⓑ sounds glamorous
- Ⓒ is very stressful
- Ⓓ builds up a person's career

5. You should stay in a new career at least five years because _____.
- Ⓐ it's your specialty
- Ⓑ you moved from one company to another
- Ⓒ you can do a good job and advance in that time
- Ⓓ the transition will be smoother

Section II Strategy Look back at the highlighted words and then do the activity below. **(3 points each)**

1. An event planner is a person who _____.
- Ⓐ helps friends
- Ⓑ sounds glamorous
- Ⓒ is very stressful
- Ⓓ arranges parties and weddings

2. To stick with it means to _____.
- Ⓐ find a specialty
- Ⓑ decide on a change
- Ⓒ stay for a few years
- Ⓓ change companies

3. A business that gets off the ground _____.
- Ⓐ is successful
- Ⓑ stays until it is clear
- Ⓒ can advance to a higher position
- Ⓓ makes a smooth transition

4. The pronoun those in paragraph B refers to _____.
- Ⓐ jobs
- Ⓑ skilled workers
- Ⓒ computers
- Ⓓ areas

5. The pronoun it in paragraph D refers to _____.
- Ⓐ another good way
- Ⓑ a new field
- Ⓒ creativity
- Ⓓ organization

Section III New Words Fill in the blanks with words from the Academic Word List from Chapter 4. **(4 points each)**

career counselors	job security	keep up with	leisure	telecommuting
on the move	outsourcing	overworked	stress	upgrade

Nowadays, workers are _____ , changing careers for many reasons. Some

            1

have lost their jobs due to _____ caused by companies searching for cheaper

            2

labor. Others feel that they are _____ , and are looking for a job with less

            3

_____. Still others need to take time off to _____ their skills

   4   5

and learn more about computers so they can _____ the latest technology.

            6

Some _____ advise people looking for work to consider several things

     7

before they accept another position. First of all, if they just lost a job, they should ask about

the _____ of the next one. Second, they should make sure they have enough

   8

_____ time so they don't feel so pressured by the demands of work. Third, they

   9

should consider _____, if possible, and working from a home office. This way,

      10

they'll have time to take courses that build their skills so they can get a better job in the future.

Section IV Building Vocabulary Find the words in the box that complete the following phrases and write them in the blanks. Each word can only be used one time. **(3 points each)**

agencies	classified	confidence	drawbacks	hopping
manufacturing	part	personnel	workforce	worldwide

1. A great number of _____ jobs have been outsourced to Asia, and factories here

   have closed.

2. To find a job quickly, go to the _____ ads of an online job board.

3. Some people enjoy job _____, while others prefer to stay at one company for many

   years.

4. To work in sales, a person needs a lot of self- _____.

5. Although mothers sometimes take _____-time jobs to stay home with young

   children, most women need to work full-time.

6. Everybody has a dream job in mind, but the reality is that all types of work have

   _____.

7. Employment _____ usually charge the company looking for workers a fee, not the

   people looking for jobs.

8. Now there are more women in the _____than ever before.

9. Many universities have a _____office where students can find work after

   graduation.

10. The decrease in manufacturing jobs is about eleven percent _____.

TOTAL ____ **/100 pts.**

Chapter 5 Test

An Ancient Art

Section I Reading Comprehension Answer these questions about the reading passage. **(3 points each)**

A Although tattoos seem like a recent fad in the United States, they actually have a long history as a form of body decoration. In some cultures, they were considered beautiful works of art. Ancient tribes in Japan and China, clans in northern Europe, and religious groups around the Mediterranean all wore tattoos. The word probably comes from *'tatu'*, meaning "to mark" in Tahitian, the language of an island in the South Pacific.

B In the 1700s, when Captain James Cook sailed from England to the South Pacific, many of his sailors got tattoos. They went back to Europe and showed them to others, and this practice became common among seamen. They enthusiastically accepted the painful experience to bring artwork back home on their bodies. From sailors, this custom gradually spread to the upper class in Europe, and in the1800s, it was a custom for rich gentlemen to travel to the Pacific islands and Asia to get tattooed by famous artists. In fact, many of the males in the royal families of Europe—princes and kings—had tattoos.

C At that time, tattooing was still done by hand, that is, artists made tiny holes in the skin with a needle or other sharp object. Then they put ink of different colors into the holes, according to a design. Nowadays, artists use electric tattoo machines, which make hundreds of holes at once, automatically pushing the ink into the skin. What used to be a long painful process takes much less time, although it still hurts! After a few days, depending on the size of the tattoo, the skin heals, or gets better, and the tattoo can be distinguished.

D In the past decade, many young people in the United States have started getting tattoos, bringing this ancient art form to life again. A third of Americans in their 20s have tattoos, while a fourth of those in their 30s have them. Tattoos are more common in Western countries, where about 20% of the population has at least one tattoo. Is this a trend or just a fad? If we look at history, we can probably call it a long-term fad. In the 19th century, tattoos were fashionable for a few decades, and who knows? They may continue to be popular for many years to come. (382 words)

1. Tattoos were popular among _____.
- (A) ancient tribes
- (B) island cultures
- (C) European royalty
- (D) all of the above

2. Captain Cook's sailors got tattooed in _____.
- (A) Asia
- (B) England
- (C) the Pacific islands
- (D) Europe

3. Gentlemen, princes, and kings were tattooed by _____.
- (A) artists doing work by hand
- (B) Captain Cook
- (C) electric tattoo machines
- (D) sailors

4. Nowadays, getting a tattoo _____ than before.
- (A) hurts more
- (B) is faster
- (C) is less painful
- (D) is more distinguished

5. In the United States, _____ have tattoos.
- (A) 25% of people in their 20s
- (B) 20% of people in their 30s
- (C) more than half of people in their 20s and 30s
- (D) a third of all people

Section II Strategy Look back at the reading and match Column A with Column B. **(3 points each)**

Column A

_____ **1.** heals

_____ **2.** needle

_____ **3.** is painful

_____ **4.** popular

_____ **5.** royal family males

_____ **6.** sailors

_____ **7.** Tahitian

_____ **8.** tattoo

_____ **9.** travel

_____ **10.** upper class

Column B

a. fashionable

b. form of art

c. rich gentlemen

d. gets better

e. hurts

f. language of a South Pacific island

g. princes and kings

h. sail

i. seamen

j. sharp object

Section III New Words Fill in the blanks with words from the Academic Word List from Chapter 5. **(3 points each)**

competitive edge	enthusiastic	expensive	influenced	invest
profits	slang	suddenly	survive	trend

The popularity of tattoos did not _____ into the 20th century; it slowed

1

down and continued only among soldiers and sailors. These men _____ each

2

other to get tattooed to show how strong they were. As a result, the general public, began

to think of people with tattoos as from the lower classes. However, in the late 20th century,

a new _____ appeared as young people started to get tattooed. This body

3

art _____ began to appear in unusual places, not only on arms, but also on

4

legs and backs. Tattoo artists began to _____ in new equipment, ink, and

5

designs. To keep their _____, they opened shops in fashionable places where

6

they could make greater _____. Actors and musicians got "tats," and many

7

_____ words came into use. As people became more _____

8   9

about this form of body art, tattoos became more _____ because patterns,

10

or "flash," were more complex. Despite this enthusiasm, however, the trend has begun to slow

down, and soon it may be a thing of the past.

Section IV Building Vocabulary Add a suffix to the words below. In some cases, two suffixes are possible. **(2 points each)**

Noun	Verb	Adjective	Adverb
-ess	-ate	-less	-ly
-ship	-ize		
-ism	-en		

1. frequent _____

2. hope _____

3. individual _____

4. soft _____

5. special _____

6. friend _____

7. host _____

8. patriot _____

9. particip _____

10. worth _____

Write the root words after the prefixes below to make one word. **(1 point each)**

Prefix	Root Word

11. com _____   _____ safe

12. counter _____   _____ bination

13. pre _____   _____ flect

14. re _____   _____ vent

15. un _____   _____ clockwise

TOTAL _____/100 pts.

Chapter 6 Test

Volunteering in the United States

Section I Reading Comprehension Answer these questions about the reading passage. **(3 points each)**

A Volunteering is a practice that many people in the United States engage in at some point in their lives. It means doing unpaid work for or through an organization. It may be a simple activity, like school children cleaning up their neighborhood park, or teenagers washing cars to earn money to support their team. It may be an educational activity, like college students tutoring children after school, or professionals advising recent university graduates. It may also be for environmental organizations, like Earthwatch or Greenpeace. Whatever a person's interest, there are dozens of ways to volunteer, and many Americans do it.

B The Department of Labor collects information on volunteering in the United States, and it says that every year, over 65 million people offer their services. One-fourth of men and one-third of women work for at least one organization without being paid. The organizations that they volunteer for the most are (1) religious, (2) educational and youth services, and (3) social and community service. People between the ages of 35 and 55 tend to volunteer a great deal, but teenagers also volunteer at lot, possibly because this type of work is emphasized in schools.

C The average time spent in unpaid activities is about 50 hours per year. Retired people (over 65) offer more of their time than other age groups—over 90 hours per year. Married people tend to volunteer more than single people, and parents tend to volunteer more than adults without children. Parents are more likely to get involved in schools and sport teams, while adults without children are more likely to offer their time to hospitals or community service organizations.

D Regarding the type of work they do, people with higher levels of education are more likely to do tutoring, coaching, supervising, and counseling, or to provide management or medical assistance. Those with lower levels of education are more likely to collect, prepare, distribute, and serve food. People with full-time jobs are less likely than those with part-time jobs to volunteer. Among those who volunteered in the past but no longer do so, lack of time is the main reason, followed by health/medical problems, and family responsibilities. All in all, the trend of volunteering is alive and well in the United States, with more people lending a hand every year. (377 words)

1. Volunteering may take the form of _____.

- Ⓐ cleaning up a park
- Ⓑ washing cars
- Ⓒ tutoring children
- Ⓓ all of the above

2. The number of Americans who volunteer is over _____.

(A) 65 million

(B) 55 million

(C) 50 million

(D) 35 million

3. _____ volunteer more than _____.

(A) children / adults

(B) married people / single people

(C) teenagers / retired people

(D) men / women

4. The most common type of organization to volunteer for is _____.

(A) social

(B) educational

(C) religious

(D) sports

5. In the United States, _____ people are offering their services.

(A) not very many

(B) the same number of

(C) less and less

(D) more and more

Section II Strategy Circle the answer that you can infer from the statement. **(3 points each)**

1. Whatever a person's interest, there are dozens of ways to volunteer, and many Americans do it.

(A) Some people are not interested in volunteering.

(B) There are many different organizations that people can volunteer for.

(C) Many Americans volunteer in a dozen organizations.

(D) It is interesting to find a dozen ways of volunteering.

2. One-fourth of men and one-third of women work for at least one organization without being paid.

(A) Women and men volunteer in equal numbers.

(B) More men than women volunteer.

(C) More women than men volunteer.

(D) Women and men work for many organizations.

3. Retired people (over 65) offer more of their time than other age groups—over 90 hours per year.

(A) Older people work more unpaid hours than younger people.

(B) Older people can only work 90 hours per year.

(C) All retired people are over 65.

(D) All retired people have more time than other age groups.

4. Regarding the type of work they do, people with higher levels of education are more likely to do tutoring, coaching, supervising, counseling, or provide management or medical assistance.

(A) People with more education like teaching and sports.

(B) People with more education like to direct other people.

(C) People with more education know how to do medical work.

(D) People with more education volunteer in areas where they can use the skills they have learned.

5. Among those who volunteered in the past but no longer do so, lack of time is the main reason, followed by health/medical problems, and family responsibilities.

- (A) People stop volunteering mainly because they don't have time.
- (B) People stop volunteering for dozens of reasons.
- (C) People stop volunteering because they get sick of it.
- (D) People stop volunteering because they have big families.

Section III New Words Fill in the blanks with words from the Academic Word List from Chapter 6. **(3 points each)**

areas	benefits	created	gap	get around
obstacles	on their own	priority	required	take their time

A volunteer organization that is very popular with young people in their 20s and 30s is Big

Brother/Big Sister (BB/BS). It is a community service organization that matches up boys and

girls with mentors, or young men and women who spend time with them once or twice a

month. Children who come from large families or those with only one parent at home may

face _____ . Their parents may not spend time with them because they
       1

work long hours. The children may be alone after school or be _____ to
                                                                2

take care of younger siblings. The young men and women who volunteer to be mentors

_____ getting to know their Little Brother or Sister. They make it a
       3

priority to _____ town with their "Littles," as they're called, and show
              4

them many different things, like museums, malls, and musical performances. They make it a

_____ to spend time with them learning something new, or just having fun. The
       5

age _____ doesn't matter, because if a person is young at heart, he or she can
       6

do anything. The _____ of the BB/BS program are sometimes surprising. After
                    7

getting a Big Brother or Sister, kids seem to do well in so many _____.
                                                                   8

Their schoolwork gets better, their self-image improves, and they look toward the future with

hope. A special bond is _____ with their mentor, which may last a lifetime.
                          9

These "Littles" go from being _____ to having a companion, and are helped and
                                10

cared for by fun-loving volunteers.

Section IV Building Vocabulary Fill in the blanks with the correct form of the participle.
(3 points each)

Dear Grandma,

My Big Sister took me to Disney World in Orlando for summer vacation. I was so

_____ (excite) when she told me we were going. We flew to Florida, and the
                    1

plane ride was _____ (excite). I had never been on a plane before! When
                                      2

we got there, we stayed at a hotel with a swimming pool. The first day I swam a lot, so I was

really _____ (tire) that night. The next day, we got up early and went to
                    3

DisneyWorld on a bus. In the Magic Kingdom, there were rides for children, so it was very

_____ (relax). Then we went to Splash Mountain, which wasn't for little
                    4

kids. At first I was _____ (frighten) as we rode around the mountain in a
                                      5

boat. All of a sudden, we were at the top and falling down! I screamed and held on to my Big

Sister. But when we splashed into the water, I laughed. It was so much fun that we went again,

and it was _____ (thrill). Another _____ (frighten) ride
                    6   7

was Space Mountain. We went up and down and around on a small train in the dark. I was

_____ (terrify) the first time—and the second time, too! It was the most
                    8

_____ (terrify) ride I've ever been on. But then, we went back to the hotel and
                    9

ate dinner by the pool. We both felt very _____ (relax) after our day at Disney
                                                          10

World. I'm so glad my Big Sister took me there!

Love,

Latisha

Write a word from Column B in Column A to form an idiom from Chapter 6. **(2 points each)**

A

B

11. hold _____

world

12. in the market _____

back

13. out of this _____

eye

14. private _____

down

15. track _____

for

TOTAL _____ /100 pts.

Chapter 7 Test

Elephant Communication

Section I Reading Comprehension Answer these questions about the reading passage.
(3 points each)

A Researchers at Stanford and Cornell Universities are studying communication patterns of the savannah, or plains elephants, and forest elephants of sub-Saharan Africa. They have made many audio and video recordings, matching the sound and behavior of the elephants in order to understand the meaning from observed patterns.

B Their findings are that elephants use many senses to communicate: sight, smell, taste, hearing, and touch. For example, when two female elephants greet each other after a long separation, they stand side by side, flapping their ears, touching and smelling each other with their trunks, making rumbling sounds. The longer they've been separated, the louder and more demonstrative they act when they meet again.

C Elephant rumbling is a low, infrasonic sound of 12–20 Hertz (Hz) that humans cannot hear. (Human range is between 20–20,000 Hz.) Researchers have divided this rumbling into three main signals: contact, "Let's go," and mating. The contact call is used by elephants that are miles away to communicate their location to other herds. All day, female leaders rumble to other groups, who rumble back. They stay far apart to ensure enough food for all the members and later meet at a watering hole and greet each other.

D Another type of rumbling is the "Let's go" signal of a head female when she wants to leave a place after drinking or resting. Facing the direction she wants to go, she rumbles until the others begin to answer and follow her. The third type is the mating rumble that a male in musth emits. Females in a herd usually answer him, although none of them may be receptive, because they mate only once every four years. However, when the male hears them, he travels to the group to assess the situation.

E A final interesting form of communication among elephants is the way they act toward their dead. If they come upon elephant bones, they stand around touching the skulls and tusks with their trunks. When researchers left the bones of other large animals, like rhinos or buffaloes, in these places, elephants examined them briefly, but they touched only the elephant remains. In India, where elephants are often killed by trains, other elephants come to the scene to caress and mourn the dead ones. (374 words)

1. Researchers are studying elephants in order to _____.
   - (A) count how many occupy a certain area
   - (B) determine how much they eat and drink
   - (C) make movies of them to show in cinemas
   - (D) understand their communication patterns

2. When female elephants greet each other after a long separation, they _____.

- Ⓐ answer in unison and look for a male
- Ⓑ demonstrate their excitement at meeting again
- Ⓒ rumble and walk away
- Ⓓ wag their trunks and tails

3. Elephant rumbling has _____.

- Ⓐ individual meanings, depending on the elephant
- Ⓑ no meaning
- Ⓒ only one meaning
- Ⓓ several meanings

4. The word emits in paragraph D probably means _____.

- Ⓐ hears
- Ⓑ perceives
- Ⓒ produces
- Ⓓ sees

5. The word remains in paragraph E is closest in meaning to _____.

- Ⓐ bones
- Ⓑ leaves
- Ⓒ leftovers
- Ⓓ stays behind

Section II Strategy Look back at the words in italics and quotation marks in the passage. Then do the activity below. **(3 points each)**

1. Rumbling is a type of elephant _____.

- Ⓐ vocalization
- Ⓑ body language
- Ⓒ symbol
- Ⓓ smell

2. An infrasonic sound is one that is _____.

- Ⓐ too high for humans to hear
- Ⓑ too low for humans to hear
- Ⓒ too high for elephants to hear
- Ⓓ too low for elephants to hear

3. The "Let's go" rumble might be given when the lead elephant _____.

- Ⓐ has finished resting or drinking
- Ⓑ greets another elephant
- Ⓒ is eating
- Ⓓ is sleeping

4. An elephant in musth is looking for another elephant _____.

- Ⓐ to attack
- Ⓑ to mate with
- Ⓒ to greet
- Ⓓ to play with

5. Elephants caress with their _____ .

   Ⓐ ears

   Ⓑ feet

   Ⓒ tails

   Ⓓ trunks

Section III New Words Fill in the blanks with words from the Academic Word List in Chapter 7.
(3 points each)

brains	gender	gestures	mammals	prey
shed light on	species	subjects	trails	vocalizations

Elephants are the world's largest land _____ , weighing 5 to 7 tons, with

_____ weighing up to 12 pounds. They travel in groups based upon

    2

_____ , with the females of several generations forming one type of group,

    3

and young males forming another. Older males, or bulls, usually travel alone except when in

musth. Elephant _____ form ancient paths through the continents of Africa

    4

and India. Zoologists used to think that there were only two _____ of elephants

    5

in the world, African and Asian. However, as researchers studied _____

    6

on the savannahs and in the forests of Africa, they discovered that these regional types

were genetically different. They also found that the elephants' _____ and

    7

_____ convey diverse messages. For example, ear flapping among females

    8

indicates friendly behavior, but among males, it indicates aggressive behavior. Different rumbles

also convey different meanings. Although other animals do not _____ upon

    9

adult elephants, their numbers are declining because of ivory hunters and deforestation.

Hopefully, current elephant communication studies will _____ how animal

    10

protection groups can acoustically monitor herds in certain areas and plan for conservation.

Section IV Building Vocabulary In the parentheses after each word, list the part of speech (*n.* = noun; *v.* = verb; *adj.* = adjective; *adv.* = adverb). Then complete the sentences that follow with the appropriate words. **(4 points each)**

1. assess (   ), assessment (   )

A bull elephant will _____ a herd of females to find a mate.

If his _____ is that none of the females is receptive, he will look for another herd.

2. confirm (   ), confirmation (   )

A lead female makes a contact call for _____ that other groups are in the area.

When she receives a response, she _____ it.

3. demonstration (   ), demonstrative (   )

Elephant communication patterns are a _____ of elephants' intelligence.

When two female elephants meet after a short separation, they are less _____.

4. record (   ), recording (   )

Researchers are making audio and video _____ of elephants' behavior.

For the past few decades, they have _____ different types of rumblings.

5. rumble (   ), rumbling (   )

When an elephant _____ , it could be sending one of several different signals.

The _____ of a female who wants to leave a place is answered by her companions

TOTAL _____/100 pts.

Chapter 8 Test
Silk Production

Section I Reading Comprehension Answer these questions about the reading passage. **(3 points)**

A   Silk was not the main product traded on the network of caravan trails connecting East Asia to the Mediterranean Sea. Despite this fact, the German explorer, Baron Ferdinand von Richthofen, gave the Silk Road this romantic name, perhaps because it was a mysterious product. Silk-making began in China in the 3rd century B.C.E., but the process was kept a secret for several hundred years. When the Chinese merchants began trading this beautiful fabric, other countries were eager to learn how it was made.

B   In the 3rd century C.E., methods of dyeing (coloring), and weaving (making cloth), were developed in a few countries along the trade routes using raw silk thread from China. In the 6th century C.E., the ruler of Constantinople asked two monks (holy men) to bring back silkworms from China. Although this was forbidden, they packed them in their bamboo canes and returned to Constantinople. There, silk production flowered and spread to Europe.

C   France and Italy became centers of the European silk industry in the 15th century until a plague killed most of the silkworms in the 19th century. In the meantime, Japan had developed modern methods of making silk and soon became the world's largest producer. In the 20th century, South Korea and Thailand developed their silk industries as well.

D   Sericulture, or silk production, involves cultivating thousands of tiny eggs that hatch into larvae (small worms) and feed on mulberry leaves. When the larvae grow into caterpillars (large worms), they make a cocoon (capsule) from a continuous thread that comes from the mouth and wraps around the body. Then the cocoons are steamed to kill the caterpillars and taken apart by unwinding the silk threads and twisting them together to make them stronger. Centuries ago, this work was done by hand by girls and women in silk factories, but now, it is done by machines.

E   Boiling raw silk produces a lighter fabric , and the cloth can be treated with different substances so that it feels and looks different. A variety of dyeing and weaving methods produce exquisite cloth that can be made into articles of clothing. Common items include blouses, shirts, scarves, and ties of pure silk. Sweaters, jackets, coats, and hats can be made by combining silk with stronger materials for warmth. The cloth can also be used for curtains, cushions, or wall hangings in houses as decorations . (389 words)

1. People wanted to learn how to make silk because _____.
- Ⓐ it was a mystery
- Ⓑ China kept it a secret
- Ⓒ silkworms were forbidden
- Ⓓ the fabric was so beautiful

2. The secret was finally brought to the West by _____.
- Ⓐ the ruler of Constantinople
- Ⓑ two monks traveling from China
- Ⓒ Chinese merchants
- Ⓓ Baron Ferdinand von Richthofen

3. The Mediterranean centers of the silk industry were _____.
- Ⓐ South Korea and Thailand
- Ⓑ China and Japan
- Ⓒ Italy and France
- Ⓓ Constantinople

4. Silk is produced by _____.
- Ⓐ tiny eggs
- Ⓑ worms
- Ⓒ girls and women
- Ⓓ machines

5. Most silk fabric is made into _____.
- Ⓐ articles of clothing
- Ⓑ dyeing and weaving
- Ⓒ stronger materials
- Ⓓ decorations

Section II Strategy Look back at the reading and find words with similar meanings. Then match Column A with Column B. **(2 points each)**

Column A	Column B
_____ **1.** caterpillars	**a.** capsule
_____ **2.** cocoon	**b.** cloth
_____ **3.** decorations	**c.** coloring
_____ **4.** dyeing	**d.** curtains, wall hangings
_____ **5.** fabric	**e.** food for silkworms
_____ **6.** larvae	**f.** holy men
_____ **7.** methods	**g.** industry
_____ **8.** monks	**h.** large silkworms
_____ **9.** mulberry leaves	**i.** making cloth
_____ **10.** network of caravan trails	**j.** mystery

_____ **11.** plague   **k.** sickness

_____ **12.** production   **l.** silk-making

_____ **13.** secret   **m.** Silk Road

_____ **14.** sericulture   **n.** small silkworms

_____ **15.** weaving   **o.** ways

Section III New Words Fill in the blanks with words from the Academic Word List from Chapter 8.
(3 points each)

archaeologist	architecture	calligraphy	caves	depicted
frescoes	mausoleum	mosque	mummies	statues

9/19/09

Dear Françoise,

I'm on a camel tour with my classmates on part of the Silk Road, and it's really exciting! At first

it was hard to ride a camel, but after a few days, I got used to it. Now it's more comfortable.

Yesterday we went into some mountain _____ that had pictures called
                                                    1

_____ on the walls. The paintings _____ scenes of daily life in
        2   3

ancient times. Today we're visiting a _____ in a Muslim town. The
                                              4

_____ of the building is simple, but the Arabic _____ on the
        5   6

walls inside is very beautiful. Our guide is an _____ who is teaching us a lot
                                                        7

about the history and culture of the Silk Road. Tomorrow, we'll stop at a _____
                                                                                    8

where dead bodies were kept. There are huge carved _____ representing those
                                                                9

who died, and there are even a few _____ inside. I've never seen one, so I think
                                            10

it will be interesting. Then we'll camp in an oasis for the night. I'm learning so much on this trip.

Wish you were here!

Your cousin,

Jacques

Section IV Building Vocabulary Fill in the blanks with the correct words in these phrases.
(2 points each)

1. _____ brief, it was a wonderful trip.

2. Caravans traveled _____ town _____ town.

3. _____ end, he decided to study archaeology.

4. Robbers contributed _____ the disappearance of some art.

5. Silk was made _____ the 15th _____ the 19th century in

    Europe.

6. The artifact was _____ the shape _____ a pitcher.

7. The Silk Road was a network _____ trails.

Choose the appropriate word for each sentence. **(1 point each)**

8. The cowry shells were _____ (beautiful/ good-looking).

9. The arabesques are _____ (attractive/ handsome).

10. The sick girl lost 20 pounds; she was _____ (slim/emaciated).

11. The big jar of spices is _____ (chubby/heavy).

12. The 300-pound man was _____ (obese/plump).

TOTAL ____ /100 pts.

Chapter 9 Test

Disabilities

Section I Reading Comprehension Answer these questions about the reading passage.
(2 points each)

A Down syndrome (DS) is a genetic disorder caused by an extra chromosome. Humans normally have 23 pairs of chromosomes, or 46; however, people with DS have 47. These infants typically have a wide face, short neck, slanted eyes, and are mentally retarded, that is, with low intelligence. They are likely to have kidney or heart problems, and adults rarely live beyond 50 years, but they are generally happy people with optimistic personalities.

B It is possible for a woman of any age to have a baby with DS, but it occurs more often in older women. For all women, the rate is one baby with DS out of 800 born, but this increases to one out of 80 for women over 35. So doctors suggest that women in this age group get tested for the condition if they become pregnant. Besides DS, there are several other disabilities that are caused by "mistakes" in our genes.

C Years ago, children with disabilities couldn't attend public schools or get jobs. They usually went to institutions where they were kept for the rest of their lives. However, attitudes have changed in recent decades, thanks to parents with disabled children. In 1975, a law called Individuals with Disabilities Education Act (IDEA) was passed in the United States. This law stated that all children with physical and mental disabilities had the right to an education, so schools were required to offer classes to meet their needs. Colleges began offering courses in "special education" to train teachers in new methods.

D This change in attitude made it possible for children with disabilities to get an education. Parents formed support groups, helping each other find good schools, recreation activities, and sports centers for their children. No longer were these children kept at home or in institutions. They could go to school with normal children and learn—and later be trained to do simple work and earn money. They could then live in group homes and support themselves like other people.

E In 1968, the Special Olympics, a competition for children and adults with disabilities, were held for the first time in Chicago, Illinois, with 1,000 participants. Today they are held every other year, with 2.25 million athletes participating in 150 countries around the world. People with disabilities are no longer ignored or institutionalized; they are part of a lively community of special people who are now able to contribute to society. (400 words)

1. People with Down syndrome _____.
- (A) have a wide face
- (B) have slanted eyes
- (C) are mentally retarded
- (D) all of the above

2. More babies with DS are born to _____.

- Ⓐ women of any age
- Ⓑ women over 35
- Ⓒ women over 80
- Ⓓ over 800 women

3. IDEA, the law passed in 1975, stated that _____.

- Ⓐ all children with disabilities had a right to an education
- Ⓑ some schools were required to offer special classes
- Ⓒ colleges had to teach special education
- Ⓓ teachers had to learn new methods

4. Because of special education, children grew up and _____

- Ⓐ could support themselves
- Ⓑ had to be kept at home
- Ⓒ had to be kept in institutions
- Ⓓ had to learn as much as normal children

5. The Special Olympics _____.

- Ⓐ is always held in Chicago
- Ⓑ has 1,000 participants
- Ⓒ has millions of participants
- Ⓓ was held once in 1968

Section II Strategy For each statement below, write *fact* or *assumption*, according to the presentation of information in the reading selection. **(3 points each)**

1. _____ Down syndrome is a genetic disorder caused by an extra chromosome.

2. _____ There is physical evidence of DS, like slanted eyes and a wide face.

3. _____ Adults with DS don't live long because of heart and kidney problems.

4. _____ Women over the age of 35 have a higher chance of having a baby with DS.

5. _____ Pregnant women over 35 always get tested for DS.

6. _____ Children with disabilities had to live in institutions before 1975.

7. _____ All children with disabilities must be educated today.

8. _____ Most people with disabilities live in group homes.

9. _____ The Special Olympics are only for people with disabilities.

10. _____ These games are held in many countries around the world today.

Section III New Words Fill in the blanks with words from the Academic Word List from Chapter 9. **(3 points each)**

cognitive	colleagues	identity	intuition	involved
maturation	memory	neuroscientist	psychologist	researchers

7/17/07

Dear Rosemary,

As you know, I've been looking for my identical twin sister for years, and I finally found

her! Just as psychologists predict, we have many similarities. As you know, I've been

_____ with work on the science of the brain. As a _____ I've

       1   2

studied long-term _____ , or how adults remember events from childhood.

                               3

Well, my sister is a _____ studying the same area, but with children. She wants

                                 4

to find out how memory changes with _____ , or how the early memories of

                                                    5

children and teenagers differ. We met by accident at a conference on _____

                                                                         6

science. There were many _____ there, and one of my _____

                                              7   8

from the institute told me she had seen a woman who looked exactly like me. I went to the

room where this woman was giving a presentation. I didn't want to bother her, so I hid my

_____ by sitting in the back. Her presentation was interesting, and afterward,

                              9

I went to the front of the room. She looked at me without saying a word—then we just hugged

each other. She said that her _____ told her that we'd find each other soon. It's

                                            10

incredible, but I feel like I've known her all my life. She's coming to my house for dinner now; we

both love to cook. More later!

Your friend,

Connie

Section IV Building Vocabulary Circle the correct word in each sentence. **(3 points each)**

1. A region in the hypothalamus is larger in (heterosexual / homosexual) men than in women and gay men.

2. The brain is divided into two (atmospheres / hemispheres).

3. When we dream, we sometimes have (insights / outsights) about our lives.

4. It is possible to have (pressed / repressed) memories.

5. Child- teenager- adult: this is the (chronology / geology) of a human life.

6. The word (vibraphone / telephone) means to "hear at a distance."

7. A (microscope / microwave) allows us to see small organisms.

8. A man who has many wives is a (bigamist / polygamist).

9. Some people who meditate practice (Buddhism / Buddhist).

10. We have 23 pairs of (homophones / chromosomes).

TOTAL _____ /100 pts.

Chapter 10 Test
The Graduation Ceremony

Section I Reading Comprehension Answer these questions about the reading passage.
(2 points each)

A   Graduating from college is a rite of passage from adolescence to adulthood for many young people. After finishing high school, teenagers begin their studies and emerge from the university as young adults. At first, they may not be sure of what to study, but after two years, they decide on a major. Then they have to take the required courses and get good grades. If they pass all their exams, they receive a bachelor's degree.

B   The graduation ceremony marks the culmination of four years of study, and most universities require students to wear a cap, a kind of "hat," and a gown, a kind of robe. This type of dress was common in the 13th century when people wore it to keep warm in cold buildings. Now students wear it only at graduation, and each college has special colors that identify not only their players at sports events but also their graduates.

C   A few weeks before graduation, students rent or buy a cap and gown from the university. They send invitations to family and friends to join them in celebrating the end of several years of hard work. On the big day, the graduates march into an auditorium or onto a football field in their colorful robes often to the music of "Pomp and Circumstance" by Sir Edward Elgar. Famous people give speeches to encourage the graduates to use their education for the good of society. They receive diplomas stating that they have earned a degree, and the university president officially declares them graduates. While proud parents wipe tears from their eyes, graduates begin cheering and tossing their caps in the air on this happy occasion.

D   At some universities, it is common for graduating students to plan "pranks," or acts that are not usually permitted. These range from simple ones—like putting soap in a campus fountain to make bubbles—to complex ones, like putting a car on the roof of a building. In 2006, students from the Massachusetts Institute of Technology (MIT) went to the California Institute of Technology (CalTech) and "stole" a famous symbol. It was a cannon weighing 1.7 tons that had been used in the Spanish-American War. MIT students delivered it to their campus 3,000 miles away where they proudly displayed it—until some CalTech students came to "rescue" it a week later and take it home. (391 words)

1. Students can graduate from college if they _____.
   - (A) put soap in the fountain
   - (B) march to music
   - (C) steal a cannon
   - (D) pass their exams

2. Students wear caps and gowns today because _____.

- (A) it is cold in the buildings
- (B) it is a tradition
- (C) they are colorful
- (D) they are warm

3. Families want to celebrate the graduates' _____.

- (A) pranks
- (B) tears
- (C) cheering
- (D) hard work

4. An example of a simple prank is _____.

- (A) putting a car on the roof
- (B) stealing a cannon
- (C) putting soap in a fountain
- (D) returning a cannon

5. Next time, CalTech may _____.

- (A) plan a prank at MIT
- (B) take back their cannon
- (C) transport the cannon to Spain
- (D) rescue MIT students

Section II Strategy For each statement below, write *fact* or *opinion*, according to the presentation of information in the reading selection. **(3 points each)**

1. _____ The majority students are adolescents when they begin college and young adults when they finish.

2. _____ It's impossible to decide what subject to study when you're 18.

3. _____ Nowadays, students don't like to wear caps and gowns.

4. _____ Graduating students usually invite their families to the ceremony.

5. _____ The speeches that famous people give at the ceremony are boring.

6. _____ Diplomas state that students have earned a degree from the university.

7. _____ Most graduates are sad to leave college and get a job.

8. _____ Some students plan pranks around the time of graduation.

9. _____ Stealing a cannon and transporting it 3,000 miles is a complex prank.

10. _____ Students who carry out pranks should be punished.

Section III New Words Fill in the blanks with words from the Academic Word List from Chapter 10. **(3 points each)**

ask for	coming-of-age	corporation	guidance	negotiations
previous	proposal	regain	rite of passage	vision

4/14/08

Dear Julio,

It's been five years since we graduated, but I still miss my old friends from college. That's

why the reunion of the Class of 2003 this summer is going to be great! The years at Central

State University were the best years of our lives. It was a _____ period
                                                                              1

in which we were growing from adolescence to adulthood. We were leaving behind our

_____ friends from high school and finding new ones in college. We were trying
        2

to decide who we were and what we wanted to do, to develop a _____ for the
                                                                              3

future. We took courses and looked for _____ from our professors, hoping
                                                  4

they would help us decide on a profession. I remember a _____ from one of
                                                              5

my professors; she said that how much money you made wasn't as important as how much

better you made the world. At first, I was just concerned about paying back my student loans

to the bank. I wanted to_____ a sense of independence, of not owing money
                              6

to anyone. When I paid them back, I remembered my professor's advice about contributing to

society. I decided to work for a nonprofit _____ . I got a job with Fair Trade,
                                                  7

an organization that buys food products, like coffee, from small farmers. These farmers can't

_____ high prices because they produce small crops. So Fair Trade holds
        8

_____ with food companies so that they pay fair prices to the farmers. I even
        9

went to Central America to visit these farms, which was like a _____ for me. I
                                                                        10

realized how much I really have and how much I must give back to society.

Your friend,

Shawn

Section IV Building Vocabulary Circle the correct word in each sentence. **(3 points each)**

1. A diploma is (inspired / inscribed) with a student's name.

2. People who attend the same university have a common spirit, or (esprit de corps / esprit de mort).

3. When a group of people share a certain, usually traditional, set of beliefs, we say they are (orthosox / orthodox).

4. Students who study hard are usually (productive / inductive) later in life.

5. If a man has two wives, he is considered a (bigamist / polygamist) in some countries.

6. The process of breathing is called (perspiration / respiration).

7. In a trial, the (proceedings / decedents) are recorded by a court secretary.

8. Romeo and Juliet had a love that was (remorseful / immortal).

9. A college student's record of courses and grades is called a (postscript / transcript).

10. During a funeral in some cultures, the (corpse / corporation) is burned.

TOTAL ____ /100 pts.

Chapter 1 Test Answer Key

Section I

1. A 2. B 3. B 4. D 5. A

Section II

1. D 2. B 3. C 4. B 5. D

Section III

1. creative 2. primary 3. involves 4. lecture
5. assignments 6. methods 7. culture 8. traditions
9. contrasts 10. goal

Section IV

1. attend 2. at 3. to 4. On/other 5. of 6. to 7. take
8. in/on

Chapter 2 Test Answer Key

Section I

1. B 2. D 3. A 4. A 5. C

Section II

1. h 2. j 3. f 4. g 5. i 6. c 7. e 8. a 9. d 10. b

Section III

1. environment 2. transportation 3. global
4. residents 5. method 6. established 7. predict
8. focused 9. access 10. solve

Section IV

1. differ 2. differently 3. pollution 4. polluted
5. predict 6. predictably 7. safety 8. safe 9. solution
10. solvable 11. different 12. predictable 13. solution
14. pollute 15. safely

Chapter 3 Test Answer Key

Section I

1. A 2. C 3. D 4. B 5. A

Section II

1. C 2. C 3. A 4. A 5. D

Section III

1. common knowledge 2. item 3. influenced
4. success 5. funds 6. grants 7. sport utility vehicle
8. capacity 9. economy 10. consumes

Section IV

1. *n.* 2. *adj.* 3. *adj.* 4. *n.* 5. *adj.* 6. *n.* 7. *n.* 8. *adj.*

9. *adj.* 10. *n.* 11. Marketers 12. offensive
13. dissatisfaction 14. information 15. advantage
16. identical 17. violent 18. subsidiary 19. influential
20. social

Chapter 4 Test Answer Key

Section I

1. B 2. D 3. C 4. A 5. C

Section II

1. D 2. C 3. A 4. B 5. B

Section III

1. on the move 2. outsourcing 3. overworked
4. stress 5. upgrade 6. keep up with 7. career
counselors 8. job security 9. leisure
10. telecommuting

Section IV

1. manufacturing 2. classified 3. hopping
4. confidence 5. part 6. drawbacks 7. agencies
8. workforce 9. personnel 10. worldwide

Chapter 5 Test Answer Key

Section I

1. D 2. C 3. A 4. B 5. C

Section II

1. d 2. j 3. e 4. a 5. g 6. i 7. f 8. b 9. h 10. c

Section III

1. survive 2. influenced 3. trend 4. suddenly 5. invest
6. competitive edge 7. profits 8. slang 9. enthusiastic
10. expensive

Section IV

1. frequently 2. hopeless 3. individualism/individually
4. soften/softly 5. specialize/specially 6. friendship/
friendly 7. hostess 8. patriotism 9. participate
10. worthless 11. combination 12. counterclockwise
13. prevent 14. reflect 15. unsafe

Chapter 6 Test Answer Key

Section I

1. D 2. A 3. B 4. C 5. D

Section II

1. B 2. C 3. A 4. D 5. A

Section III

1. obstacles 2. required 3. take their time 4. get around 5. priority 6. gap 7. benefits 8. areas 9. created 10. on their own

Section IV

1. excited 2. exciting 3. tired 4. relaxing 5. frightened 6. thrilling 7. frightening 8. terrified 9. terrifying 10. relaxed 11. hold back 12. in the market for 13. out of this world 14. private eye 15. track down

Chapter 7 Test Answer Key

Section I

1. D 2. B 3. D 4. C 5. A

Section II

1. A 2. B 3. A 4. B 5. D

Section III

1. mammals 2. brains 3. gender 4. trails 5. species 6. subjects 7. gestures 8. vocalizations 9. prey 10. shed light on

Section IV

1. *v.*, *n.*, assess, assessment

2. *v.*, *n.*, confirmation, confirms

3. *n.*, *adj.*, demonstration, demonstrative

4. *v.*, *n.*, recordings, recorded

5. *v.*, *n.*, rumbles, rumbling

Chapter 8 Test Answer Key

Section I

1. D 2. B 3. C 4. B 5. A

Section II

1. h 2. a 3. d 4. c 5. b 6. n 7. o 8. f 9. e 10. m 11. k 12. g 13. j 14. l 15. i

Section III

1. caves 2. frescoes 3. depicted 4. mosque 5. architecture 6. calligraphy 7. archaeologist 8. mausoleum 9. statues 10. mummies

Section IV

1. In 2. from/to 3. To this 4. to 5. from/to 6. in/of 7. of 8. beautiful 9. attractive 10. emaciated 11. heavy 12. obese

Chapter 9 Test Answer Key

Section I

1. D 2. B 3. A 4. A 5. C

Section II

1. *fact* 2. *fact* 3. *assumption* 4. *fact* 5. *assumption* 6. *assumption* 7. *fact* 8. *assumption* 9. *fact* 10. *fact*

Section III

1. involved 2. neuroscientist 3. memory 4. psychologist 5. maturation 6. cognitive 7. researchers 8. colleagues 9. identity 10. intuition

Section IV

1. heterosexual 2. hemispheres 3. insights 4. repressed 5. chronology 6. telephone 7. microscope 8. polygamist 9. Buddhism 10. chromosomes

Chapter 10 Test Answer Key

Section I

1. D 2. B 3. D 4. C 5. A

Section II

1. *fact* 2. *opinion* 3. *opinion* 4. *fact* 5. *opinion* 6. *fact* 7. *opinion* 8. *fact* 9. *fact* 10. *opinion*

Section III

1. coming-of-age 2. previous 3. vision 4. guidance 5. proposal 6. regain 7. corporation 8. ask for 9. negotiations 10. rite of passage

Section IV

1. inscribed 2. esprit de corps 3. orthodox 4. productive 5. bigamist 6. respiration 7. proceedings 8. immortal 9. transcript 10. corpse

Reading Strand Placement Test
Vocabulary Section

Vocabulary I Choose the best word to complete each sentence. **(2 points each)**

Example: Brazil and Argentina are the largest _____ in South America.
  - (A) categories
  - (B) cities
  - (C) countries
  - (D) neighborhoods

1. No one lives with Rosa in her apartment. She lives _____.
  - (A) alone
  - (B) lonely
  - (C) only
  - (D) together

2. Tom's family has 3 children, Amy's family has 3 children, Reina's family has 2 children, and Ben's family has 2 children. The _____ number of children in these families is 2.5.
  - (A) small
  - (B) average
  - (C) equal
  - (D) total

3. When teachers speak too softly and rapidly, it is _____ for their students to understand them.
  - (A) easy
  - (B) little
  - (C) different
  - (D) difficult

4. In many cultures, women do most of the _____. For example, they clean the floors and wash the clothes for their families.
  - (A) farming
  - (B) homework
  - (C) housework
  - (D) cooking

5. Mr. Lee's restaurant is successful because he always waits on his _____ politely and serves them wonderful meals.
  - (A) customs
  - (B) customers
  - (C) consumers
  - (D) users

6. In a basketball game, two teams _____ against each other to score points by throwing a ball into a basket.

- Ⓐ compete
- Ⓑ cooperate
- Ⓒ complete
- Ⓓ exercise

7. In this country doctors usually have high _____ , or position in the society.

- Ⓐ profession
- Ⓑ situation
- Ⓒ state
- Ⓓ status

8. Many companies in the computer industry were started by very young people. For example, Bill Gates was only twenty years old when he and Paul Allen _____ the Microsoft Corporation in 1975.

- Ⓐ based
- Ⓑ discovered
- Ⓒ located
- Ⓓ founded

9. _____ up to 20% is customary in U.S. restaurants. Some places even add 15% to the bill for all parties of six or more.

- Ⓐ Waiting
- Ⓑ Tipping
- Ⓒ Buying
- Ⓓ Eating

10. I wouldn't go to the new mall just yet. If you can _____ another week or two, until the Grand Opening is over, the crowds will be much more manageable.

- Ⓐ hold out
- Ⓑ hold up
- Ⓒ wait on
- Ⓓ hold onto

Vocabulary II Read each item and then answer the vocabulary question below it. **(2 points each)**

Example: The city government recently announced plans to build a new road through Mountain Dale, a beautiful neighborhood on the south side of the city. The residents of Mountain Dale are angry about the road. Yesterday a group of them went to a meeting at City Hall to express their *views* on the city's plans.

Which of the following is closest in meaning to *views* as it is used above?

- Ⓐ pictures
- Ⓑ opinions
- Ⓒ sights
- Ⓓ beautiful scenery

1. The brain is divided into many parts. Each part serves specific and important functions. The cerebrum is the largest and most complex *area* of the brain. It controls thought, learning, and many other activities. Which of the following is closest in meaning to *area* as it is used above?
   - (A) the size of a surface, calculated by multiplying the length by the width
   - (B) a particular subject or group of related subjects
   - (C) a particular part or section
   - (D) a part of an activity or a thought

2. By studying the pyramids of Egypt, researchers have learned a great deal about ancient Egyptian *culture*. They have discovered, for example, that different social classes existed even in the earliest cities. Which of the following is closest in meaning to *culture* as it is used above?
   - (A) activities that are related to art, music, and literature
   - (B) a society that existed at a particular time in history
   - (C) a scientific experiment of people from a particular country
   - (D) education of people in a certain social group

3. Timothy is going to ride his bike around the world. In order to see all the countries and sights he wants to, before he begins his adventure, he will *map* his route. Which of the following is the closest in meaning to *map* as used above?
   - (A) to pack bags for a trip
   - (B) to plan the path of a trip
   - (C) to prepare a bicycle for a trip
   - (D) to talk about something

4. With today's computer networks, the *transmission* of data from one place in the world to another can happen instantly. Which of the following is closest in meaning to *transmission* as it is used above?
   - (A) the process of working together on the same computer network
   - (B) a job that involves traveling from one place to another
   - (C) the set of parts of a vehicle that take power from the engine to the wheels
   - (D) the process of sending information using electronic equipment

5. Roger has some annoying tendencies. For one thing, he's *inclined* to talk about himself and his achievements. Which of the following is closest in meaning to *inclined* as it is used above?
   - (A) bending forward to say something
   - (B) likely to do something or behave in a particular way
   - (C) holding a particular opinion
   - (D) talking a lot about the same thing

6. At medical centers throughout the United States, researchers are *conducting* investigations into the causes of heart disease. Which of the following is closest in meaning to *conducting* as it is used above?
   - (A) carrying out an activity or process in order to get information or prove facts
   - (B) directing the playing of an orchestra, band, etc.
   - (C) carrying something like electricity or heat to cure heart disease
   - (D) guiding or leading someone somewhere

7. In recent years, it seems that headlines and articles about war and violence have *occupied* the front pages of newspapers everywhere.

Which of the following is closest in meaning to *occupied* as it is used above?

(A) taken up time

(B) lived in a place

(C) controlled a place by military force

(D) filled a particular amount of space

8. Studies in public schools have shown that *exposure* to art and music has many benefits for children. It improves their literacy, critical thinking, and math skills.

Which of the following is closest in meaning to *exposure* as it is used above?

(A) a situation in which someone is not protected from risk or danger

(B) attention that someone gets from newspapers, television, etc.

(C) the chance to experience something

(D) the act of showing something that is usually hidden

9. Ronald and James are roommates in a university dormitory. They have frequent arguments because Ronald prefers to go to sleep early and James always stays up late. Also, Ronald likes quiet while he studies, but James insists that loud music helps him concentrate. How can James and Ronald *resolve* these conflicts?

Which of the following is closest in meaning to *resolve* as it is used above?

(A) make a definite decision to do something

(B) solve again using new techniques

(C) gradually change into something else

(D) find a satisfactory way of dealing with a problem or difficulty

10. It is important that students learn to read and write before they go to college. In particular, they need to practice reading on their own and learn how to write a *succinct* and logical argument.

Which of the following is the closest in meaning to *succinct* as used above?

(A) taking a long time to explain

(B) correct

(C) original

(D) clearly and concisely expressed

Reading Section

Directions: Read each passage and answer the questions below it. **(2 points each)**

Reading Passage I

A How do you react to the taste of different foods, like coffee or lemon? Do they have a flavor that you like? Or do they taste very strong to you? Why do people react differently to different flavors?

B We all know that different people have different food preferences. Researchers have discovered some reasons for these differences. Your culture and your life experience are partly responsible for your preferences for certain foods. Your food preferences are also partly genetic. (Your genetic preferences are the ones that you were born with.) In order to discover people's genetic preferences, researchers use a chemical called PROP. People taste it and respond to the taste. To some people, PROP has no flavor. The researchers classify these people as "nontasters." To other people, the flavor of PROP is a little bitter, or sharp. These people are "tasters." Then there are the people who can't stand the flavor of PROP. They find it to be unbearably bitter. These people are the "supertasters." Tasters have more taste buds on their tongues than nontasters do, and supertasters have many more taste buds than tasters do. This explains why supertasters are more sensitive to PROP and to the flavors in certain foods. So if you think the flavors in coffee, grapefruit juice, and broccoli are very strong, you may be a "supertaster."

Example: The topic of the reading passage is _____.
- (A) the flavor of coffee
- (B) becoming a supertaster
- (C) differences in people's taste sensitivity
- (D) research in the flavor of different foods

1. The main idea of the reading is that _____.
- (A) there are people who like different foods
- (B) there are cultural and genetic reasons for the differences in people's food preferences
- (C) some foods have a very strong flavor
- (D) PROPs can be used to identify different types of tastes

2. The meaning of *genetic* preferences is _____.
- (A) preferences for certain foods
- (B) preferences researchers have discovered
- (C) the preferences of some people
- (D) the preferences that people are born with

3. What is PROP?
- (A) a chemical
- (B) something that people are born with
- (C) a discovery
- (D) a researcher

4. Why do researchers use PROP?

    (A) because it has no flavor

    (B) to find out the responses to foods people were born with

    (C) to discover the flavors in certain foods

    (D) because people like its flavor

5. A food that is bitter has _____.

    (A) no flavor

    (B) little flavor

    (C) a coffee flavor

    (D) a sharp flavor

6. People who _____ are classified as *supertasters*.

    (A) can't stand the flavor of PROP

    (B) think that PROP has no flavor

    (C) think that PROP tastes a little bitter

    (D) like bitter flavors

7. Taste buds are probably _____.

    (A) tiny pieces of food

    (B) the small bumps on the surface of people's tongues

    (C) chemicals in food that give it its flavor

    (D) something in broccoli, grapefruit juice, and coffee

Reading Passage 2

A   After a cold, snowy winter, many people look forward to the long hot days of summer. The normal heat of summer can be pleasant. However, it's important to be aware that excessive—that is, too much—heat can be dangerous. There are other summer weather dangers, for example, tornadoes, lightning, and floods, but excessive heat kills more people each year than any of these. According to meteorologists (weather scientists), a heat wave is a period of excessive heat that lasts two days or more. A heat wave stresses people and can cause illnesses. These illnesses include heat cramps, heat exhaustion, and heat stroke. The people who are at the greatest risk during heat waves are the elderly, babies, and those with serious diseases.

B   High humidity (moisture in the air) can make the effects of heat even more harmful. As humidity increases, the air seems warmer than it actually is because it's more difficult for the body to cool itself through the evaporation of perspiration. During heat waves, meteorologists use the heat index to determine the level of danger. The heat index measures how hot it really feels when high humidity is added to the actual air temperature. As an example, if the air temperature is 95° F (Fahrenheit) and the humidity is 35%, the heat index is 98° F. But if the air temperature is 95° F and the humidity is 70%, the heat index is 124° F. Doctors say that even young, healthy people can die of heat stroke if they exercise outside when the heat index is high. During a heat wave, it's best to take it easy, drink plenty of water, and stay out of the heat as much as possible.

1. The main idea of Paragraph A is that _____.
   - (A) people look forward to the long hot days of summer
   - (B) too much heat can have dangerous effects
   - (C) tornadoes, lightning, and floods are dangerous
   - (D) meteorologists can define heat waves

2. The main idea of Paragraph B is that _____.
   - (A) humidity is moisture in the air
   - (B) meteorologists use the heat index during heat waves
   - (C) high humidity increases the danger of high air temperatures
   - (D) it's important to stay inside during a heat wave

3. The word *excessive* means _____.
   - (A) too much
   - (B) important
   - (C) long
   - (D) coming in waves

4. In the passage, lightning is mentioned as an example of _____.
   - (A) excessive heat
   - (B) a storm
   - (C) a stress on people
   - (D) a summer weather danger

5. A meteorologist is _____.
   - (A) a doctor
   - (B) a weather scientist
   - (C) a space scientist
   - (D) a dangerous weather condition

6. The heat index measures _____.
   - (A) the amount of moisture in the air
   - (B) air temperature
   - (C) a person's body temperature
   - (D) the temperature the body feels when heat and humidity are combined

7. Based on the information in the passage, which statement is true?
   - (A) Young, healthy people are more likely to die from excessive heat than elderly people are.
   - (B) The elderly, babies, and people with serious diseases are most likely to die from excessive heat, but it can kill young, healthy people, too.
   - (C) Perspiration is a dangerous effect of excessive heat.
   - (D) All heat waves include high humidity.

8. Why did the author write this passage?
   - (A) To warn people about the dangers of excessive heat and give suggestions about avoiding them.
   - (B) To give people useful information about the weather in the summer.
   - (C) To describe the work of meteorologists and their use of the heat index.
   - (D) To let people know how the body can cool itself naturally.

Reading Passage 3

A   Even though education is compulsory (required by law) for children in the United States, it is not compulsory for them to go to a conventional school to get that education. In every one of the 50 states, it is legal for parents to educate their children at home, or to "home school" their children. Although no state requires parents to have special training to home school their children, the regulations parents must follow vary widely from state to state. New Jersey, for example, imposes virtually no requirements. In contrast, New York requires home schoolers to notify their school districts, file instructional plans and frequent reports, and submit the results of tests or other forms of assessment for each child.

B   Increasing numbers of American families have been opting for home schooling. According to the National Center for Educational Statistics, about 1.1 million children were being home schooled in the spring of 2003. This represents an increase from the 850,000 who were being home schooled in the spring of 1999. In addition, the home-schooling rate—the percentage of the school-age population that was being home schooled—increased from 1.7 percent in 1999 to 2.2 percent in 2003.

C   A survey conducted in 2003 asked parents to give their most important reasons for home schooling their children. Thirty-one percent cited concerns about the environment in conventional schools, including safety, drugs, or negative peer pressure. Thirty percent said that the most important reason was to provide religious or moral instruction. Sixteen percent said that the most important reason was dissatisfaction with academic instruction at conventional schools. Parents gave other reasons, too; for instance, many said that they wanted to strengthen family bonds or allow their children more freedom.

D   It is difficult to show whether conventional schooling or home schooling works better. Home-schooled children tend to score significantly higher than the national average on college entrance tests. But educators say that it isn't easy to determine how meaningful the figures are, given the complexities of making direct comparisons. In the debate about home schooling, socialization is more of an issue than achievement. Advocates of conventional education believe that home-schooled children are at a disadvantage because they miss out on the kinds of social interaction and relationships with peers that are an essential part of a total education. Advocates of home schooling say that home-schooled children are not socially isolated; they think that home-schooled children have a larger social structure because they can be out in the world, in contact with people of different ages, and having experiences that they could never have in conventional schools.

Directions: For each question, choose the best answer based on the reading passage.

1. The word *conventional* means _____.

   (A) relating to a meeting

   (B) following what is normal or usual

   (C) following a religion

   (D) educational

2. According to the passage, increasing numbers of American families are choosing home schooling. What information does the author give to support this statement?

   (A) In every one of the 50 states, it is legal for parents to educate their children at home.

   (B) Thirty-one percent of parents say that the most important reason for home schooling is concerns about the environment in conventional schools.

   (C) The number of children who were being home schooled increased from 850,000 in 1999 to about 1.1 million in 2003.

   (D) A survey was conducted in 2003.

3. Scan (look quickly through) the passage to find the answer to this question: How many of the parents surveyed in 2003 said that the most important reason for home schooling their children was dissatisfaction with academic instruction at conventional schools?

   (A) 1.1 million

   (B) 30 percent

   (C) 16 percent

   (D) 2.2 percent

4. Three of the following statements give facts, and one gives an opinion. Based on the reading passage, which one is the opinion?

   (A) Home-schooled children are at a disadvantage because they miss out on some kinds of social interaction and relationships.

   (B) Thirty percent of parents who home school their children said that the most important reason was to provide religious or moral instruction.

   (C) The home-schooling rate increased from 1.7 percent in 1999 to 2.2 percent in 2003.

   (D) The regulations that parents of home schoolers must follow vary widely from state to state.

5. Which paragraph gives information about the number of home-schooled children who attend college?

   (A) Paragraph B

   (B) Paragraph C

   (C) Paragraph D

   (D) That information is not given in the passage.

6. In Paragraph D, the author implies, but does not state directly, that _____.

   (A) home-schooled children tend to score significantly higher than the national average on college entrance tests

   (B) it should be easy to make direct comparisons between conventional and home schooling

   (C) parents are not academically qualified to teach their children

   (D) there is controversy about the benefits of home schooling

7. Based on Paragraph D, we can conclude that advocates of conventional education object to home schooling mainly because home-schooled children _____.

   (A) cannot achieve academically

   (B) cannot be compared to conventionally educated children

   (C) are not well socialized

   (D) have too much freedom

Reading Passage 4

A   In recent years, the game of golf and golf tourism have grown in popularity in many places in the world. Golf, which traces its roots back to 15th century Scotland, is often viewed as a pleasant and harmless way to relax in a natural setting. But golf courses are not natural developments. They are artificial constructions that have a big environmental impact. As a result, there is often controversy about the building of golf courses.

B   Opponents of the use of land for golf courses bring up a number of environmental concerns. One is that a golf course covers a great deal of land, typically up to 200 acres, and in the process of developing this land into a golf course, it is common for fragile native ecosystems such as wetlands, rainforests, or coastal dunes to be destroyed. Indigenous grasses, shrubs, and trees are removed and replaced by foreign vegetation. The construction process causes soil erosion and results in the loss of biodiversity and habitat for wildlife. Another concern is the amount of chemical pesticides, herbicides, and fertilizers used to maintain the grass on a golf course once it is established. These chemicals can result in toxic contamination of the air, the soil, the surface water, and the underground water, and this in turn leads to health problems for people who live near the course or downstream from it, for people who work at the course, and even for the golfers. Yet another concern is that golf courses require an enormous amount of water every day. Their water consumption can lead to depletion of scarce fresh water resources. These and other concerns about golf courses have provoked protests, most recently in east and southeast Asia, against planned golf projects.

C   Designers, developers, and operators of golf courses have become increasingly aware of the environmental issues and of the protests. Consequently, they have sponsored research into more environmentally sensitive ways of constructing and maintaining courses. They believe that it is possible to build golf courses which protect and preserve the natural features of the landscape and natural habitats for wildlife. Their suggested practices include using native trees and shrubs, planting types of grass that require less water and are best adapted to the local climate, and using reclaimed water. Proponents of golf courses believe that these "green" golf courses can actually provide environmental benefits to their sites.

D   However, even a "green" golf course is likely to result in some environmental degradation and loss of habitat. Therefore, many biologists and wildlife ecologists, such as Lawrence Woolbright, a professor at Siena College in Albany, New York, contend that the best places to construct new golf courses are places that are already degraded, such as former landfills (garbage dumps) and old industrial sites, rather than on undeveloped land. A golf course that transforms a degraded site into a scenic landscape with wetlands and woodlands and habitat for wildlife could actually be a benefit to the environment.

1. Which of the following is the best statement of the main idea of the reading passage?
- Ⓐ   Golf courses are artificial constructions, and are often built with no regard for the environment.
- Ⓑ   Controversies about golf courses affect the tourist trade.
- Ⓒ   Golf courses have significant effects on the environment, and these effects lead to controversy.
- Ⓓ   Golf and golf tourism are growing in popularity internationally, leading to a more negative effect on the environment.

2. What word is opposite in meaning to the word *indigenous*?
   - (A) native
   - (B) foreign
   - (C) natural
   - (D) vegetation

3. Which of the following is *not* mentioned in the passage as a negative environmental impact of a golf course?
   - (A) the destruction of fragile native ecosystems
   - (B) soil erosion caused by cutting down trees
   - (C) pollution caused by traffic and maintenance equipment
   - (D) depletion of scarce fresh water resources

4. Which of the following best summarizes the environmental concerns of opponents of the use of land for golf courses?
   - (A) They are concerned about the amount of land that a golf course covers.
   - (B) They are concerned about the impact of the process of constructing new golf courses.
   - (C) They are concerned about the impact of the maintenance of established golf courses.
   - (D) All of the above.

5. Based on Paragraphs C and D, we can infer that a "green" golf course is one that _____.
   - (A) consumes a great deal of water
   - (B) is environmentally sensitive
   - (C) is new and not degraded
   - (D) has grass, shrubs, and trees

6. Based on the information in Paragraph C, we can conclude that _____.
   - (A) it is certain that "green" golf courses have already been built
   - (B) it is certain that "green" golf courses will be built in the future
   - (C) it is not certain that any "green" golf courses have already been built or will be built in the future
   - (D) opponents of golf courses accept the idea that "green" golf courses can actually provide environmental benefits to their sites

7. Based on Paragraph D, we can infer that the author of the passage _____.
   - (A) agrees with Lawrence Woolbright
   - (B) disagrees with Lawrence Woolbright
   - (C) is willing to accept some environmental degradation and loss of habitat
   - (D) is opposed to all golf courses

8. What would be an appropriate title for this reading passage?
   - (A) A Brief History of Golf
   - (B) Golf's Dirty Side
   - (C) Why Make Golf Green?
   - (D) The Beauty of Golf

Answer Key for Reading Strand
Placement Test

Vocabulary I

1. A 2. B 3. D 4. C 5. B 6. A 7. D 8. D 9. B 10. A

Vocabulary II

1. C 2. B 3. B 4. D 5. B 6. A 7. D 8. C 9. D 10. D

Reading Passage 1

1. B 2. D 3. A 4. B 5. D 6. A 7. B

Reading Passage 2

1. B 2. C 3. A 4. D 5. B 6. D 7. B 8. B

Reading Passage 3

1. B 2. C 3. C 4. A 5. D 6. D 7. C

Reading Passage 4

1. C 2. B 3. C 4. D 5. B 6. C 7. A 8. C

SCORING FOR INTERACTIONS/MOSAIC READING PLACEMENT TEST	
Score	**Placement**
0–40	Interactions Access
41–55	Interactions 1
56–70	Interactions 2
71–85	Mosaic 1
86–100	Mosaic 2

This is a rough guide. Teachers should use their judgment in placing students and selecting texts.